The Silver Bullet:
How RFPs are won

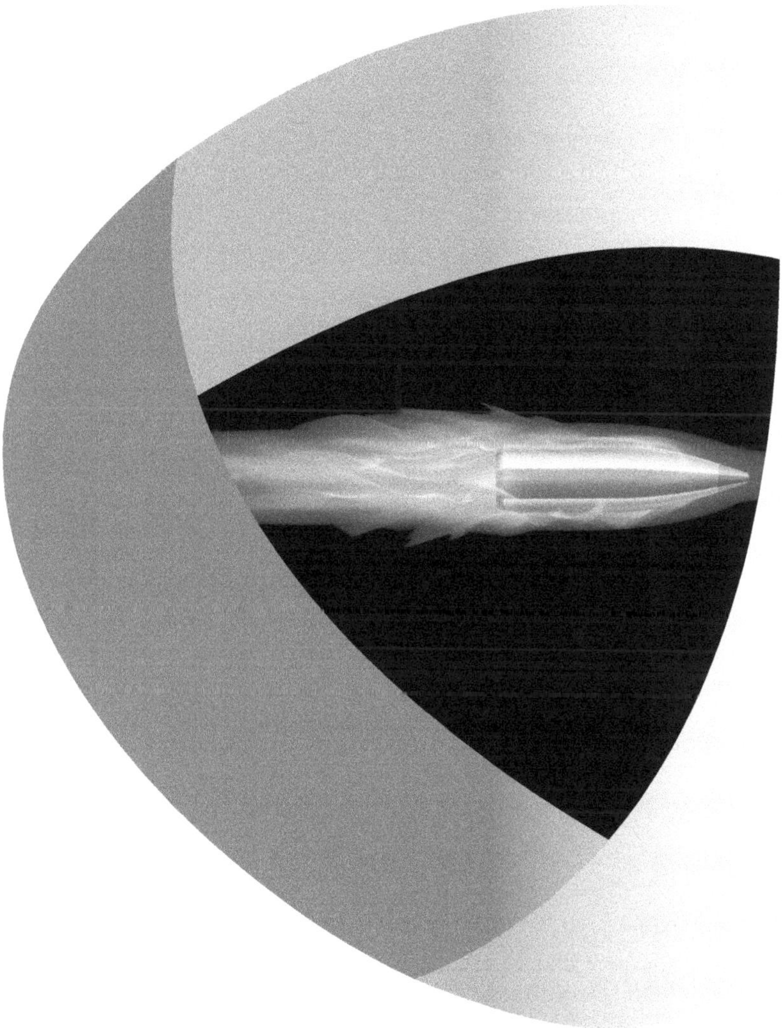

NANCEY L WATSON

Commissioning editor
Alex Davies

Editorial assistant
Francesca Ramadan

Published by
Globe Law and Business Ltd
3 Mylor Close
Horsell
Woking
Surrey GU21 4DD
United Kingdom
Tel: +44 20 3745 4770
www.globelawandbusiness.com

ISBN: 978-1-78358-336-2
A catalogue record for this book is available from the British Library

Contents

Contents

Executive summary

When I tossed around ideas for titles for my book, I thought of many involving winning and strategy, but then I thought of the silver bullet. I wondered if I dare call my book the *silver bullet*; after all, aren't we all looking for that? I would have said that there is no such thing, but that was before I created my workshop, *Strategic Proposal Management*© 2017, 2018. I have helped professional services firms win over $3 billion in bids. They often ask me, "How do you come up with these strategies?" I remember telling them that if I could bottle it – and sell it – I would. I can't explain how I think. It just comes to me. It was after facilitating this workshop with all sizes of law firms in several countries that it crystallized. I decided that there really is a silver bullet. I have used this customized workshop as the basis for this book because all firms and proposal writers are looking for the silver bullet to win more Request for Proposals (RFPs).

This book is not intended to be followed to the letter on every proposal. To be honest, sometimes you are given such a short deadline that the best you can do is get it out the door on time. This strategic guide is meant for you to refer back to when you come across areas where you need reminders of when to apply a certain strategy. The information is not meant to overwhelm. It presents best practices in an ideal world. It is meant to get you thinking about how to plan strategically through every phase of the proposal process. Having said that, writing proposals is not a linear process, so you may need to skip around to find the section you need at the appropriate time.

The book opens with a factor that is often overlooked – the impact legal procurement has in influencing law firm selection. I have hosted the seminar "How Procurement Impacts Law Firm Selection and Performance Measurement" in Toronto, New York, Houston, and Los Angeles. Every time I am amazed at the wealth of information I learn. Attendees are surprised at the growing sophistication of in-house legal departments and procurement professionals. I am now accredited to present courses for Continuing Professional Development and

Continuing Legal Education on this topic. Please read this first chapter on legal procurement with care. I hope you will find it insightful.

Chapter two outlines questions firms should ask before they decide to propose for the work. I strongly believe that the go/no-go decision is the most important step in the proposal process and in my experience it is often the step that is ignored. By constantly trying for long shots you demoralize the proposal team and waste valuable time that could be put towards a real opportunity. Before diving into your next proposal, review the checklist to see if it is a viable opportunity.

Analyzing the RFP – or what I like to call the "cheat sheet" – is key to winning. All sorts of gems are hidden beneath the surface, just waiting to be dug up and explored. Chapter three goes into these buried treasures.

It is critical to work well with subject matter experts to pry out of them the key selling points. Even after over 30 years of writing proposals all I can say is that I *help* clients win proposals. I need their dedication and specialized knowledge to write a compelling proposal. I also need their desire to win. Chapter four, on working strategically as a team, is as important for proposal managers as it is for lawyers and subject matter experts. Teams working in sync provide great proposal strategies.

I started my career as a researcher for a leading management consulting firm and I have carried that skill with me ever since. I realized early on that research is the key to knowledge. One time I researched seven products to be considered by a prominent food manufacturer and they chose five of the seven products that I recommended. I was only in my mid-20s at that time and I thought anyone could have done this! One of the things I stress in chapter five is that you must do your "homework" if you want to get the edge in winning proposals. And yes, I believe anyone can do it.

Kick-off meetings centred on strategy are a key component of the proposal process, and are the subject of chapter six. The kick-off meeting is not the best time to select lawyers to serve the client. Hopefully that is done beforehand, leaving time to identify win themes when the team gets together. Good preparation for the meeting allows proposal professionals to demonstrate their value. Kick-off meetings should be held for formal and informal RFPs. I wouldn't miss this step, even if it is a brief strategy discussion with the lead partner.

This dovetails nicely with chapter seven on different strategies for proposal sizes and timelines. You can't be a rock star on every proposal, and sometimes you need to hit unreasonably tight deadlines to get it done on time. This chapter will help you differentiate what you can do to be strategic for different kinds of bids.

In chapter 8 we start getting down to the nuts and bolts of a compelling proposal – needs, solutions, outcomes, and proof. Without proof that you can deliver on your promises, all the strategy discussions in the world will not win the tender. As you are building your credibility you need to back up everything with the proof that you have done this kind of work successfully before, and can do it again.

This leads to differentiation, explored in chapter nine. Yes, it could be part of the preceding chapter, but I wanted to keep it separate so it wouldn't get lost in the minutia. Years ago, I would have said that there is not much differentiation between law firms. That is not true today. Some law firms are known for their high technology, processes, and/or pricing savvy. It may take competitive research (my favorite thing) and several brainstorming sessions to distill your differentiators, but it will be well worth it.

Writing a strategic executive summary is the subject of chapter 10, although it could well be the first chapter. The school of thought is that you should start with the executive summary and have the proposal flow from that. The executive summary is where you accentuate the needs, outcomes, solutions, and proof that you are the right firm to hire. In the ideal world, I agree with this philosophy; however, I also know that sometimes you just have to dive in, start getting words on paper, and write the executive summary in hindsight. The summary is a very important part of your proposal because it is the only thing that is read by the C-Suite (other than the pricing section, that is). This is where you get to say what you want to say because you don't have to follow a question and answer format.

Chapter 11 looks at how to effectively use red teams to verify strategies. A red team is an independent group that challenges the proposal team to improve the proposal by assuming the role of the client. Red teams can be a strong influence in winning as they can be objective and draw attention to missing strategies.

The book concludes, with chapter 12, on strategic proposal tracking. You can use information on the number of wins and losses, the reasons why you won or lost, pricing, the proposal team, and how much time was spent on each bid to build your strategies going forward. This information will also help to drive go/no-go decisions in the future.

I hope by now you have identified the silver bullet – *strategy* at every step in the proposal process. I look forward to hearing from you as your win rate increases.

About the author

Nancey L Watson, BEd. is president of NL Watson Consulting Inc. She has helped professional services firms win over $3 billion in competitive bids. For nearly three decades she has worked with Big Four accounting firms, Top 10 engineering firms, and since 2012 has worked almost exclusively with global, national, mid-size, and boutique law firms in Canada and the United States on proposals and presentation strategies.

She is an internationally recognized speaker who presents on topics such as pricing tactics, pricing masterclass, legal procurement's impact on law firm selection at in-house and law firm conferences including Thomson Reuters, Law Firm Marketing Partner Forum, Canadian Corporate Counsel Association National Conference and In-House Counsel World Summit, LawVision Group, Practice Partners Roundtable, and Legal Marketing Association, Eastern Canada Regional Conference.

Nancey is the creator and facilitator of the workshop: Strategic Proposal Management© 2018. The training session results in proven strategies on how to increase win rates in today's highly competitive marketplace.

She is also the presenter of the Accredited Continuing Professional Development/Continuing Legal Education Course, How Procurement Impacts Law Firm Selection. As a contributing author for Thomson Reuters Legal Executive Institute she has articles published on procurement and law firm strategies and several podcasts on the Legal Executive Institute website.

Between 2008 and 2012, she acted as the membership committee chair and board member for the legal marketing association, Toronto chapter, and is presently membership committee chair for Toronto. Nancey can be reached via email at www.nlwatsonconsulting.com.

Acknowledgements

I would like to express my gratitude for the input and encouragement I received from the following legal procurement, pricing and competitive intelligence professionals: Zena Applebaum, corporate strategy, competitive intelligence, legal industry; Richard Brzakala, director of external legal services; Vincent Cordo, Jr, central legal operations officer; Stuart Dodds, co-founder/principal of Positive Pricing; Justin Ergler, director, alternative fee intelligence and analytics, global external legal relations, GSK Legal; and Jo Ellen Hatfield, a senior strategic sourcing professional.

Chapter 1: How legal procurement impacts law firm selection – a strategic approach

When I started writing proposals over 25 years ago, life was much simpler in the business world and in particular in writing responses to a Request for Proposal (RFP). The formal RFP, if it existed at all, was relatively vague and the proposals were the same. When I see a proposal from that era it is quite embarrassing to think that at the time we thought it was a good document. I sometimes wonder how we won the bid with such a general document. That would not work in today's world. RFPs have become more sophisticated and complex. In many ways I think that is a good thing. As RFPs articulate the corporation's legal needs in more detail, law firms are in a better position to prove their worth to the client or potential client. In my book I am using the term "client" to refer to both existing and potential clients to keep it simple.

Over the past several years I have noticed another significant change in the kind of RFP law firms are receiving, not just in terms of volume and complexity, but the fact that the issuer came from someone in *procurement*. This made me investigate what legal procurement specialists do and what their role is in relation to RFPs. I met with several leading-edge professionals who are responsible for global legal procurement at their companies.

I will explain in more detail later the role of legal procurement professionals; suffice to say at this point is that companies are hiring procurement specialists to help them issue RFPs, pricing of legal matters, and implementing processes internally and with law firms to increase efficiency in the delivery of legal services. Some specialists have an MBA, a black belt in six sigma, and a background in procurement, or were previously pricing managers at top law firms. Pricing professionals in law firms are advised to be ready for their new counterparts in procurement.

The procurement specialists, sometimes referred to as sourcing professionals, discussed with me the significant gap between procurement and law firms, and I recognized a need to help bridge the gap, particularly as procurement is a key influencer with respect to which law firms get the work. Legal procurement is quickly gaining traction, particularly among companies with significant legal spend. The sooner law firms understand the role of procurement, the sooner they will have a better relationship with their clients, and a better chance of winning RFPs. Justin Ergler, director, alternative fee intelligence and analytics at GlaxoSmithKline says:

> *"Law firms need to get to know the procurement professionals – when you do so, do it constructively. Procurement prefers to deal with the pricing people when negotiating pricing as they speak the same language."*

This is not to say that all companies have legal procurement professionals. Many companies still use their in-house lawyers to select their legal services providers. However, the number of major corporations with dedicated legal procurement specialists is quickly increasing. The figure could be as high as two-thirds of the Fortune 500. In addition, the number of global companies that have dedicated legal procurement professionals is growing.

Global procurement leaders from top-tier corporate industries provided me with candid commentary on what they want, need, and expect when hiring outside counsel. As a result, I have given seminars on "How Procurement Impacts Law Firm Selection" in Toronto, New York, Houston, and Los Angeles with a panel of top legal procurement specialists. I am now accredited/certified for Continuing Legal Education (CLE) and Continuing Professional Development (CPD) hours in Canada and various states in the US for courses on this topic.

I must admit that the jaws of lawyers and business development professionals tend to drop when I discuss legal procurement practices. Procurement teams work with line managers and the legal department on the content of RFPs, analyze proposals, and present their recommendations to the General Counsel for the final selection. The methodology used to analyze proposals is often quite complex. Some companies use software to help them make comparisons between the responses of the proposing law firms. It also enables them to analyze and make price comparisons between the firms. This information is often stored so that they can predict how much a matter should cost when asking for quotes for specific work.

What is a major focus for companies regarding the provision of legal services? Vincent Cordo, central legal operations manager, in an interview with Christopher Jeffery, Thomson Reuters said:

"The biggest focus for us is quantifying overall commercial value while continuously fine-tuning the process to positively impact our outcomes with appropriate, value-based pricing. We are looking for efficiencies but not at the sacrifice of quality. Processes and assignments are not taken lightly. We audit these metrics and report on how our panel firms have embraced processes that enhance the efficiency we're looking for, whether it is through budget performance, outcomes, utilization of technology, or improving workflow processes. The reporting requirements of external counsel continue to advance, so firms are expected to report on results to internal counsel with assurances of a high-quality work product at a lower cost, and on schedule. Scoring and reporting on the overall account management is also a very important component of the relationship."

I have noticed the number of RFPs for legal panels is increasing, particularly global panels. The RFPs are often handled by senior procurement specialists at corporations and global legal project managers within global law firms. It is very expensive for a company to manage the work done by numerous law firms, so they are looking for efficiency and cost savings. In 2016, Shell cut its global legal panel from 11 advisers to just six in a review that saw the company look at over 200 firms. *Legal Business* quotes Shell's legal director, Donny Ching, as saying:

"The new firms bring with them a combination of strong legal experience and expertise, global reach, and flexibility with regards to cost arrangements that will help Shell achieve a higher standard of performance for our organization, maintaining a strong and growing long-term position in the competitive environments in which we operate."

If you are not on the company's legal services panel, your chances of getting business from a company is greatly reduced because you do not have an existing relationship with the client. That is why you must win the bids now. Ergler, quoted above, adds:

"Open communication is critical in developing a strong relationship between legal counsel and procurement. Transparency is key, law firms need to give the whole response to corporate counsel and not leave anything out."

This includes back and forth communication between the legal department and the client – it goes both ways.

The role of legal procurement

We all acknowledge that one of the main roles of procurement is to lower the cost of legal spend – not necessarily to the lowest bidder, but achieving good value for the lowest possible price. Each task procurement performs is designed to achieve the desired business outcomes by ensuring that the right people are doing the right work, the right way, at the right price. Instead of just measuring hours, sourcing professionals are focusing on improving efficiency, negotiating and measuring value, setting budgets, measuring results, service levels, and overall cost. It is now "more for less".

Now there is another kid on the block that law firms need to be aware of. Cordo, quoted above, says:

> *"There is a need for understanding and collaboration between legal operations and how they partner with procurement. Many organizations have procurement groups and now they have legal operations teams. Understanding the different roles and how they can partner together creates synergies that benefit the organization. If the relationship is built the right way they can expand the opportunity; it doesn't have to be only procurement and it doesn't only have to be legal operations. Fundamentally, building a strong partnership relationship between these different functions is to accomplish the same goal – to provide ultimate value to the organization."*

Cordo explains the role of legal operations as:

> *"Legal operations supports and streamlines core legal applications, data analytics, and services – controlling outside spend, maximizing team capacity, capturing value, with focus on continuous improvements. Their role also includes leveraging in-house legal project management capabilities, coupled with sourcing team insights, and performing after action reviews on what was procured. Measuring and reporting on key performance indicators and scoring quality are key focus areas, and an incessant search for opportunities to capture value is fundamental."*

As mentioned, sophisticated procurement specialists have many software tools at their disposal. Some are created in-house and others are purchased. These tools include reverse auctions, eTendering, eEvaluation, report on performance measurement, legal spend, and the status of matters. You need to understand the tools procurement teams use in order to present a proposal that will give you an advantage when replying to RFPs. For example, if you use the client's terminology in the RFP when responding to questions, the software will pick up your responses.

Let's examine some of the key roles of procurement and what you can do to enhance your bids.

Increase the quality of legal representation

Legal procurement professionals look for lawyers and law firms who have experience with similar matters and who have the skills that are well matched for the specific legal matter. They research whether the firm has done similar work or solved a similar case and what the result was. Some RFPs ask for the names of judges or courts where the lawyer has argued similar cases. Procurement teams want to know the lawyer's track record in order to predict the possibility of a desired outcome. *Proposal writers should keep this in mind when they explain their firm and team's experience in a proposal.*

As buyers, legal procurement professionals are typically involved in the development of general purchasing strategies, sourcing processes and criteria, as well as in negotiating fees and contracts, drafting engagement letters, and terms and conditions. *Plan to work well with procurement and explain how your will work with them in your proposal.*

Implement key performance indicators

Procurement initiates key performance indicators (KPIs) such as whether a law firm delivered on time and on budget; where the pricing came in; what the end result of the matter was; and other factors, all of which get put into a performance metric that's used when evaluating the legal provider's performance. You will notice these kinds of metrics in the scoring criteria in many RFPs. *As this information is tracked by legal operations after the law firm has been engaged, make sure you put this kind of information into your proposal and discuss how you track it internally.*

My procurement contacts have informed me that the performance metrics listed below are tracked, so I suggest that you build this material into your proposals. All of these criteria can be built into your legal process management procedures and repurposed for your bids.

- **Expertise**. Track the performance of law firms and individual lawyers. *Provide data on this information, include big deals, wins, and deal closings.*

- **Quality**. Good value for work product relative to the amount of time spent and fee charged. Comparisons are made for the same type of work, the time, and fees charged by other firms. *Show value for services. Make measurable information available to your clients on invoices.*
- **Process**. Timely completion and submission of reports, scoping, and after-project reviews are tracked. *Conduct after-project debriefs with clients to ensure satisfaction and avoid misunderstandings. After-project debriefs can be conducted via an email survey following projects. If necessary, implement new processes to avoid undesirable issues arising again. Mention your processes in the proposal.*
- **Efficiency**. Tasks are completed on time; timely response to inquiries; and meeting deadlines. *Keep a record of these activities and your legal project management (LPM) processes and use them in proposals.*
- **Technology**. Current software tracks projects to see if they are delivered on time. *Describe how your software tracks projects (especially if in real time). Offer a demo or if possible attach a demo of your software program to the proposal.*
- **Budget**. Agreed upon disbursements are checked, and the project is managed within the quoted budget. *Present statistics on your track record for delivering projects within budget. Outline your process for when/if a cost-overrun is going to happen.*
- **Billing**. Matter management and billing are monitored. Adherence to corporate terms and conditions and billing guidelines is critical. *Make sure your invoices add up to value for money. Explain your billing procedures and give examples in your bids.*
- **Alternative fee arrangements**. Procurement looks at reducing the total legal spend as a percentage of revenue. Experienced legal procurement professionals can place a value on comparable Alternative Fee Arrangements (AFAs) because they track fees and quotes on various types of matters from numerous firms. This puts them in a strong position to evaluate fee quotes. *When offering AFAs in proposals do the math to make sure it shows good value for the fee. Explain why it is a good fee arrangement and show the math.*

The following is a list of various popular alternative pricing approaches. Clients are increasingly combining AFAs to create hybrid arrangements when the project is fully scoped. *Explain several choices for the client so they can select the best AFA for a particular kind of project.*

Pricing models include:

- Fixed fee;
- Phase-based billing;
- Capped fee;
- Cap and collar/risk sharing;
- Contingency fee;
- Reverse contingency;
- Success fees; and
- Holdbacks.

Procurement professionals will tell you that the bottom line in pricing boils down to asking questions, clarifying scope, and knowing your numbers. If you don't understand what procurement needs, ask. Explain the reasoning for your assumptions. You need to know your threshold, clearly understand the scope, and set milestones. You must know your true cost to set the right price. Pricing should be beneficial for both the client and the law firm rather than a zero-sum game.

Importance of billing data

Richard Brzakala, a director of external legal services, has been managing external counsel globally for nearly 20 years and has extensive experience with procuring legal services. In recent years, the pricing component of many RFPs has grown in importance for many cost-conscious clients rolling out RFPs. Brzakala commented:

> *"The level of sophistication has grown as in-house legal departments have become empowered with a plethora of billing data that is invaluable to how they manage their external counsel matters. Consequently, careful consideration should be given to answering any RFP pricing question. Where possible, any numerical values provided in an RFP should not be based on any subjective or visceral (i.e. 'gut') feelings a firm may have, but instead should be supported by real empirical data that is derived from the firm's historical experience.*
>
> *"Procurement's role is to source service providers, explore different pricing models, staffing models, and joint process improvement standards.*

> *The more you can help them do this the better standing you will have with your clients. Put it in your proposals. If you are not asked a specific question about it, put it in the executive summary – just get it in."*

Evaluate value added services

Procurement is upping the ante for value added services. Continued legal education (CLE) seminars for in-house counsel, a hotline/helpline for in-house counsel and line management, and secondments are favorites among procurement professionals. The challenge is that many "added values" are no longer differentiators, but have become expected services. Can you put a fee value on your CLE education to demonstrate the value of the course that the client is getting for free? Can you offer secondments free or at cost? Brainstorm added value offerings with lawyers and your administrative teams; you will be surprised at the ideas you come up with. For example, your technology and legal project management team may be able to offer suggestions to increase efficiency that add true value.

Procurement professionals and legal departments use a range of metrics and benchmarks in addition to price when evaluating proposals. Legal procurement regularly conducts industry benchmarking analysis, rate increase analysis, and invoice audits. At a Legal Marketing Association event a general counsel from a large financial institution said that they have a full-time employee just checking invoices, and if an invoice does not measure up to the expected performance they query it. If they have to keep asking about invoices, they stop using the firm. They do not contact the firm to let them know, they just stop using them – they have lots of firms to choose from. So, if you are not getting more work from clients, be proactive and ask why. *Put your billing processes into your proposal.*

If, for example, a litigation matter is going to go beyond the budget estimate, lawyers need to communicate with the in-house lead counsel or procurement specialist in advance to communicate *why* the matter is veering off the proposed budget and *how* the new scope has increased the time and effort required. This kind of activity goes to your performance-scorecard measurement. *Once again, put this process in your proposal.*

Information security

Information security is a growing role for legal procurement. Brzakala, quoted earlier, says:

"With all of the advantages of technology there comes risk and an obligation on the part of law firms to manage the changing face of risk, wherever it resides. Ultimately, there is no room to be a laggard when it comes to cybersecurity, as clients are increasingly demanding it. As innovation continues to change technology, and the utilization of business tools by users changes, the relevance and importance of how information security (IS) is managed by law firms is crucial. RFP questions today, unlike years ago, are the standard by which sophisticated buyers of legal services gain their first impression of where a firm is in terms of IS table stakes. Firms cannot afford to be in denial or underestimate the importance and relevance of proper IS preparedness. Ensuring clients that a firm is prepared, proactive, and committed to safeguarding their information is the foundation upon which all other components of the client–law firm relationship is built."

Client relationships

Selecting and keeping a number of external legal advisors is critical to the smooth workings of the legal department. It can also present a risk to in-house counsel and the company if the wrong firm is chosen. Decisions as to which law firms to use are not made lightly; the law firm needs to build trust in their capabilities and develop a good rapport with the legal department and line management. Yes, you need to demonstrate your worth, not only to in-house counsel, but to department managers as well.

No matter what, client relationships are still critical to getting and keeping the work. Legal procurement professionals may act as "gatekeepers" who control the flow of communication and information from the law firm to the potential client. They are, however, less likely to be the final decision-maker.

Every procurement specialist I have spoken with has emphasized that open communication is paramount, especially if something is starting to go wrong. Be proactive. Don't wait for the client to call you. General Counsel have said that they want their legal advisors to pick up the phone to discuss issues before they become problems. They also want their legal advisors to make suggestions about how to fix it.

Clients like to deal with the same people year after year because they feel comfortable that the lawyers understand their personality, processes, business, industry, and legal issues. It reduces the time spent to bring new advisors up to speed and it reassures them that their trusted counsel will know how to act. If there is a change on the team, make sure that you inform your client in advance. Introduce the new team member as soon as possible. It is also a step towards succession planning and moves the business model from "this is my client" to "this is the firm's client". Appropriately introducing new team members in a proposal to an existing client can add to the value of your proposed team.

We have discussed many items and processes that should be described in proposals. The following information will help you get into the head of procurement and create a mindset when responding to RFPs. I asked several procurement professionals what they want and don't want from law firms when responding to RFPs. Here is what they said.

What clients want:

- Client-centric thinking – it's all about them;
- Understanding the client's industry and business;
- Describe different and beneficial ways of doing things (project management etc.);
- Customized responses, especially those that demonstrate understanding of the client; and
- Questions to be answered directly and with a crisp written style.

What clients don't want:

- Lack of demonstrated knowledge of client or key industry issues;
- Stock responses (non-customized boilerplate);
- Offering the "A Team" and getting the "B Team" – companies track who was presented in the proposal and who is on the invoice;
- Vague pricing, too many caveats (e.g. for fixed fees); and
- An unwillingness to be flexible in pricing and offer alternative fee arrangements (AFAs).

Why proposals lose

I want to focus on three of the primary reasons why proposals are lost. I have conducted many debriefing interviews for clients and have found that one of the main reasons for losing a bid is a lack of understanding of the company's business. A recent study of the British legal market commissioned by LexisNexis and Judge Business School at Cambridge University stated that a stunning 40 percent of clients in the LexisNexis survey noted that *senior partners* of their law firms lacked more than a basic knowledge of their businesses.

Second, the lack of demonstrated knowledge of the client's industry is another reason why law firms are not selected. I suspect that in many instances firms are selected to propose because the client believes they have expertise in their industry sector. Is it because you did not demonstrate your industry expertise and its relevance to the client that you lost the bid?

The third reason is the lack of proven expertise; as in the previous instance, make sure your expertise is undisputable. All things being equal, price is very important to clients – but not at the expense of relevant expertise.

A parting word about working with procurement. Procurement wants law firms to respect their role and play by the rules, which means following procurement's process; providing information that procurement wants, when they want it, and how they want it. Do not try to end run them. Be professional when working with procurement, get to know them, and find ways to help them do their job more effectively.

Strategies to remember

1. Understand procurement's role and how to work with them;
2. Provide expertise and your understanding of the client's industry and business;
3. Develop processes that you can put into proposals;
4. Reference key performance indicators in your proposals; and
5. Recognize that general counsel is the final decision-maker – procurement is the gatekeeper.

Chapter 2: The go/no-go decision – strategic considerations

I strongly believe that the go/no-go decision is the most important step in the proposal process. In my experience, it is the phase that is often ignored and can result in a costly process. Everyone wants to quickly jump on board and respond to the "business opportunity". An Altman Weil study in 2008 stated that a typical proposal costs between $35,000 and $65,000. Leaping at the opportunity without analyzing it properly can result in abandoning the proposal effort after spending a lot of time on it because you later discover that you do not have the expertise to fulfill all the requirements, or you can't justify the fees you quoted to the management committee.

While RFPs are sent to numerous firms, the best position to be in is to be known to the company issuing the RFP. If you are an incumbent, you need to showcase the great work you have done for the client. However, they may be going out to bid because they are not happy with your service. In this case, you need to show how you will fix the problem. I have encountered several instances where I recommended – at my own peril – changing the team. One example was when a client slipped through the cracks during a merger. I had to tell the managing partner (who was the client relationship partner) that I thought he should select a new team lead and add some new members to the team. He agreed with the assessment and we were told during the debrief that we did not originally have a chance of winning, but because we admitted our error and changed the team, we won.

In another case, we outsourced some of our work to a firm that was located in a region where we did not have an office. Unfortunately, the firm did not provide good service and the client went out to bid. We heard about the RFP through the grapevine and asked if we could propose. The company said yes, but reluctantly. I suggested to the CEO that we form an alliance with a different firm that could do the work and explain to our client that we had changed our service provider and formed a new business arrangement with the company so that this problem would not arise again. When we were rehearsing our presentation, the team from the new firm was concerned about admitting we were previously at fault. I pointed out that in the outline for our presentation from the client they had asked, "How will you make sure that this will not happen again?" It pays to own up to mistakes and provide solutions. At the debrief, we were told that in the beginning we did not have a chance of winning, but because we had come up with a valid solution, we won the client back.

I know that many lawyers will not believe this, but the fewer RFPs you respond to, the more you will win, and the more fees you will make. Following a go/no-go decision process before starting the proposal results in wins. Part of the process is determining whether there is an existing relationship with the prospective client, geographical reach, estimated fee, kind of services, expertise and qualifications of the proposed team, and the scope of the project. I have tracked the results of win/loss reports and found that not only did the law firm's win rate go up (by not bidding on low opportunity bids) but the proposals that were won garnered a higher fee (by fitting into the law firm's wheelhouse).

There is a need to customize the go/no-go process as each firm has its own structure, local, national, global, and its own internal processes. The go/no-go procedure needs to work within the decision-making structure of the firm. The procedures below are guiding principles that will help you develop your go/no-go bid process.

You need a strict decision-making process that you can adhere to. Consider the following:

Return on investment

Financial metrics

- Win opportunity estimate, non-chargeable lawyer cost, overtime costs of proposal team, overruns of proposal budget, predicted fee value, production costs (for example, digitized proposals are expensive), and positioning against the firm's financial plan. The legal project management team needs to be notified to scope the opportunity to assist the pricing team with their fee estimate and the pricing team needs to be involved to make sure the work will be profitable.

People metrics

- Evaluation of team against required qualifications; locations team will be drawn from.

Firm metrics

- Probability of success, strategic importance, benefits of bid to firm.

Checklists and process charts

When a notification is received to respond to an RFP consider using the following checklist to make sure that the right decisions are made and the right strategies are adopted to ensure a high win rate. The objective is to determine whether the bid is a good fit for the firm, meet the practice group's business objectives and predict the likelihood that your firm will be engaged. As you go through this process you will likely add more questions to consider before proceeding to bid.

Go/no-go decision checklist

Company name:

RFP release date:

Proposal due date:

Opportunity:

Intent to bid notice date:

Mandatory meetings to attend:

Closing date for questions:

Estimated value:

Questions to consider

Yes/no analysis will help determine whether to invest your time on the bid. You may consider a rating or point system to give additional weight to your yes/no decisions.

	Yes/ no	Comments
1. What is the state of our relationship with the company? Are we the incumbent? Do we have any contacts within the company?		
2. Is there a conflict of interest with any of our existing clients?		
3. Can we meet the mandatory requirements and terms and conditions?		
4. Do we want this work?		
5. Is the timeline reasonable to put in a strong proposal?		
6. What is the financial position of the prospective client?		
7. Has the client set out transparent evaluation criteria?		
8. Can we deliver the service without straining our resources?		
9. Do we have the qualifications to do the work?		

10. Do we have other clients in this industry?

11. Is the work in line with our strategic plans?

12. Do we have a realistic opportunity of winning the work?

13. Does the RFP appear to be pre-determined?

14. Do they want to change or are they just fishing?

15. Do we have sufficient information on our competitors to assess their strengths and weaknesses? Can we differentiate ourselves from the competition?

16. Is price the only deciding factor? Will it be profitable work?

17. Can we deliver at a competitive rate?

18. Has the scope of the work been clearly defined?

19. What are the risks involved?

20. Is there any opportunity to grow our business within this company?

Go/no-go decision

Pre-determined RFPs

Not all bids are pre-determined (where the winner is decided upon in advance) and it is difficult to be certain whether the RFP is pre-determined or not. You may decide to bid and present a strong case and win – you never know.

Questions to consider that may indicate the bid is pre-determined include:

1. Is the deadline unreasonably short? Are they willing to agree to an extension?
2. Does the evaluation criteria favor the incumbent or a particular competitor?
3. Is the kind of information requested reasonable for this kind of bid?
4. Have they provided too much (overwhelming) or too little information?
5. Have they given enough information to enable a good response?

Under what circumstances would you bid for work that you are not sure whether you can win? Well, there is *one* time when I would recommend that you go for it. If you have great qualifications and want to impress the company, you may want to submit a proposal so that you will be on their radar. However, you must come in a strong second. If they allow for a debrief then you can impress them and open up an opportunity for some future work. Yes, I have seen it happen, but you need to work it.

Hopefully I have built my case for instituting a go/no-go decision process at your firm. Before leaping to respond to a pitch or RFP, take the time to analyse the opportunity. If it is a go decision – go for it with all your might.

Strategies to remember

1. The go/no-go process is the first step to undertake before bidding;
2. Determine your ROI;
3. Customize your go/no-go checklist;
4. Don't fall into the trap of bidding for a pre-determined bid; and
5. Only bid when you believe you have a fair chance of winning, unless you have a good reason for proposing.

Chapter 3:
Analyzing the RFP to identify strategies

Looking at an RFP from the client's perspective is a must when responding to RFPs. We have all heard about putting on the client's hat but actually doing it during the RFP process is another story. Due to time constraints it is often difficult to achieve. This chapter gives a bird's eye view of the RFP process from procurement's perspective.

Procurement's RFP process

To start the RFP process or tendering process (UK), in-house counsel usually evaluates their internal resources and identifies gaps in their legal expertise and timelines to handle the work. They speak with line management to assess the project as to how critical the matter is and its complexity and then determine whether or not external counsel is needed.

RFP questions must reflect the company's legal needs including relevant expertise, experience of the team, knowledge of the company and the industry, geographical reach, fees, etc. RFPs require a considerable amount of work on behalf of the corporate RFP team.

The next step is to collect information about law firms to decide what firms to invite to propose. This will likely include existing counsel but could also include other external firms. Typically, in-house counsel ask their peers or other colleagues in the industry. They then perform their due diligence by reviewing court documents, websites and legal directories. They look at the industry profile of their candidates and develop a profile of potential firms and lawyers.

As pricing is a very important element of the RFP, a lot of input will be devoted to the fee section. In-house counsel discuss their pricing requirements and criteria with the chief financial officer and/or procurement specialists to determine the kind of fee quotes they expect; this will likely include AFAs.

Once this information has been decided upon, the more sophisticated companies will create a decision-making matrix or scorecard to measure the proposals. I have included a good example of a scorecard in this chapter for your review.

After following these steps, the company is now ready to launch the RFP. It can take a lot of time to develop an RFP considering all the stakeholders that need to be consulted, particularly if it is a global bid. Therefore, it behooves us to treat the RFP with respect.

I think that receiving a formal Question and Answer RFP is like getting a gift. It's also somewhat like getting a "cheat sheet," as it becomes your proposal road map. Everything the client wants to know is laid out for you. But don't be fooled by it. You need to spend a good amount of time dissecting the RFP to find the strategies you will need to win, particularly if the RFP has two sections: 1) the technical response (response to questions) and 2) the pricing components.

A typical RFP looks much like the following:

Table of contents

1. General introduction
2. Calendar due dates
3. Response guidelines
4. Company profile
5. Project information (scope of work)
6. Service requirements
7. Team requirements
8. Mandatory requirements
9. Evaluation criteria and/or rated requirements
10. Pricing
11. Terms and conditions

On the other hand, I have seen global RFPs sent as an email message. They had a sentence about what they wanted and a few bullets with the usual: proposed team, expertise, relevant experience and fee quote. The *good news* is that with an informal bid you can pretty much write your own proposal; that is, you can say pretty well anything you want because the request is really vague – the *bad news* is that it is really hard to get a grip on the client's true needs and why they need this information. This is when you have to do your homework. You need to know what's happening with this company, what's happening in the industry, and why an RFP is important to them right now. If it is an existing client, you may already know the answers. If not, read chapter 5:

"Doing your homework to identify strategies." It makes it harder to differentiate your firm because the informal RFP is so vague. However, by researching information about the company and industry, you may be able to uncover some interesting tidbits that you can highlight in your proposal to stand out from the pack.

Another way of looking at responding to an RFP is as a "process of elimination" – the last man standing wins. This is when reviewing mandatory requirements is critical. The first step for many companies and particularly the public sector is to have administrators ensure that the proposal is compliant before the analysis takes place. Proposals that are not compliant are rejected right away.

There are several things to pay attention to in determining mandatory requirements. Other than following the obvious *Mandatory requirements* section to the nth degree, you need to watch out for words like "will," "shall" and "must" that are peppered throughout the RFP as they are also mandatory requirements.

I like to use the "Find" feature in Microsoft Word to find all the mentions of "will," "shall" and "must" and put all the mandatory requirements on a spreadsheet and use it as a checklist when reviewing the proposal to make sure nothing gets missed. This includes the requirements for the number of copies, deadlines, and delivery method.

Some RFPs require an original hard copy of the proposal. If an original document is requested, make sure that you have an original signature on the covering letter and on any forms. Remember, it is a game of elimination, so be on the safe side and overdo rather than underdo compliance.

It is also important to review the *Terms and conditions* (T&Cs). Oddly enough, I find that I am often the only one who reads the T&Cs. I am not a lawyer so I caution the lawyers to ensure that they have read them thoroughly. When I highlight sections that I think partners need to review, they usually review the entire document to make sure there are no surprises. I know that public sector T&Cs must be agreed with in order to proceed, but have found that even then there can be an exception. As I said, I read them religiously. One time I was comparing the past T&Cs with the revised T&Cs and found an interesting clause. I brought it to the CEO and general counsel's attention and lo and behold it was a *big* change. They decided not to propose and let the other firms know about the clause. All firms refused to comply. Discussions were held with the government agency and the clause was removed.

While we are on mandatory requirements, I want to remind everyone how important the delivery time is and how important it is to get a copy of your timed delivery receipt. As you know, particularly for public sector bids, the delivery time is marked in hours, minutes, and seconds. If you are *one second* late your proposal is non-compliant and your document is not opened. I worked on a bid that was worth millions and ensured it was delivered on time. I also made sure I got the delivery receipt with the time stamp from the client. In addition, I called the client to make sure the proposal was received. Yes, paranoia at its best. The client said the proposal had not been delivered. Thankfully I was able to scan the delivery receipt and email it to the client. A few hours later the client called and said that our proposal had been found on someone's desk who was on vacation for two weeks. Check, check, and double check is my motto.

Working the proposal team to complete exhaustion is not the way to put your best foot forward. Another quick example; I was working with an engineering firm and the team had worked days, nights and weekends to get an $80 million bid out. They were so tired that they missed inserting the *Scope of Work* into the document and there was no time to proofread the proposal so no one caught it. Obviously, the proposal was non-compliant. I am very thankful that it was not my proposal, but I felt really terrible for everyone involved. It is critical to follow the workback schedule that is distributed to the proposal team to avoid these painful situations. It becomes the domino effect when one deadline is missed, and in the end everyone suffers.

I would like to add one more thing about mandatory requirements as it relates to timing. Too many bids are pushed to the last second – and I mean second when they are sent by email. You must remember that emails are in a queue and just because you press "Enter" on time your bid may arrive late. If you are a lawyer working with a proposal team, please do not put them under this stress. I know the last person holding the bag gets blamed but in reality the proposal was likely off course along the way.

Now that we've made sure you won't be disqualified by missing a mandatory requirement, let's look at strategies that are hidden in the RFP.

Your win themes are buried in the RFP

I like to use highlighters when I analyze RFPs. I use pink for mandatory requirements because if you miss any your proposal is non-compliant. Next, I use green to identify strategies and yellow to highlight questions to ask the client for clarification.

Dividing up the RFP

Mandatory requirements – pink

As mentioned, mandatory requirements need to be met. Watch out for the following:

- Terms such as "must," "shall" and "will"; and
- Terms and Conditions.

Questions – yellow

Highlight areas to ask the client about if they are not clear and include any sections in the Terms and Conditions:

- Record questions to ask the client for clarification;
- Ensure partners review the questions prior to sending them to the client; and
- Review answers to the questions and ask for further clarification if necessary.

Identify strategies – green

The following are questions to consider to uncover strategies that are buried in the RFP:

- Why are they issuing the RFP now?
- What internal reasons or external reasons may influence this RFP?
- What do they need?
- What do they really want?
- What results are they looking for?
- What is/are the required service(s)?
- What is the importance of price? (Review the evaluation criteria.)
- Who is on the selection committee?
- What proof can you offer to prove that you are the best firm?

Answer the questions

One of the reasons why proposals lose is that the question is not answered in a direct and clear manner. You may think that this is not possible. However, I assure you that this is true, according to the procurement people I have spoken with and in the debriefs I conduct with clients. If you want to do a little test for yourself, go back a year or two and review an RFP and your proposal and see if you've answered all the questions directly. I think you may be surprised. As we rush through proposals, some of the information may have ended up on the cutting room floor. We need to have someone not connected with the proposal do the final proofread and check for incomplete or weak responses.

Evaluation/selection criteria

Another gift is when the RFP has detailed selection criteria. Use the client's evaluation/selection criteria to analyze the RFP and when asking partners for information and reviewing the final proposal.

Some selection criteria are rather vague, such as the following:

> **The selection criteria for this RFP will be based on a variety of factors, including but not limited to the following:**
>
> - Top talent and depth of expertise in key practice areas;
> - Knowledge of our industry;
> - Value of services (i.e., AFAs);
> - Knowledge of and experience in relevant technologies; and
> - Other value-adding and innovative recommendations.

While better than nothing, it does not provide detailed information on how the proposal will be judged because it does not have scoring or weighting criteria. If the company supplies weighted scoring criteria, use it to prioritize where to put your emphasis. Spend your time on the sections of the RFP where you will get the most points, particularly if the timeline is tight.

Procurement's scoring process

The scoring of the proposal is shared when law firms are granted a debrief with the client. Sophisticated procurement specialists use electronic scorecards to tally up the scores, whilst others do their scoring/evaluating offline. In any case, decisions are usually reached by consensus by in-house counsel, finance and/or procurement specialists. Jo Ellen Hatfield, senior strategic sourcing manager, corporate procurement, says:

"Value driven analysis incorporates a weighted methodology which ensures the most critical needs of the in-house counsel team are reflected through the scoring process."

Overleaf is an example of a scorecard that procurement uses to evaluate proposals (Fig. 1).

Winning the bid is just the beginning. Do not promise what you cannot deliver. One of procurement's tasks is to track performance on a firm level and at the lawyer level. Following the win, procurement measures delivery of services. They look for:

Quality:

- Desired results – positive outcomes (trials, mergers and acquisitions) etc.;
- Responsiveness – phone calls and emails returned in a timely manner, projects completed on time; and
- Expertise – the best lawyer at the appropriate level.

Efficiency:

- Technology – productivity;
- Communication – frequency; and
- Terms and Conditions and/or contract – compliance.

Fee commitments:

- Cost containment – no overruns;
- Cost transparency – detailed, clearly understood invoices with back-up material;
- Budget management – monitoring budget closely;
- Staffing – appropriate partner to associate ratio; and
- Competitive rates – competitive with market.

Naturally, I cannot cover everything that I put into my proposal workshop as it is a six-hour training session and is often done with a live RFP. However, this should give you a good starting point to review RFPs with strategy in mind and not just to get the proposal out the door.

ENTER INFORMATION IN GREY AREAS ONLY			SCORING		
EVALUATOR NAME:			1 Not acceptable 2 Requires some improvement 3 Meets expectations 4 Exceeds expectations 5 Significantly exceeds expectations		
Evaluation category	**Rating**	**RFP source**	**Firm 1**	**Firm 2**	**Firm 3**
Total Score			0.000	0.000	0.000
Client service	**15%**		0.00	0.00	0.00
Reporting delivery and capabilities		Section IV, subsection G, q.1-3	0.00	0.00	0.00
Service Level Agreement – Responsiveness focus		Section IV, subsection H, q.1-3	0.00	0.00	0.00
Matter budgeting process		Section IV, subsection I, q.1-4	0.00	0.00	0.00
Attorney expertise	**30%**		0.00	0.00	0.00
Attorney expertise and experience		Section III, subsection F; Section IV, subsection A, q.2-4	0.00	0.00	0.00
Geographical presence		Section IV, subsection J, q.1	0.00	0.00	0.00
Industry knowledge		Section III, subsection C, q.1-3	0.00	0.00	0.00
Conflicts management and adverse representation		Section III, subsection A, q.5-6	0.00	0.00	0.00
Firm viability and financials	**25%**		0.00	0.00	0.00
Financial stability, transition		Section III, subsection B, q.1-6	0.00	0.00	0.00
Rate/fee proposal		Section IV, subsection D, q.1	0.00	0.00	0.00
Information systems	**20%**		0.00	0.00	0.00
Data security		Section IV, subsection B, q.1-6	0.00	0.00	0.00
System backup and recovery		Section IV, subsection C, all	0.00	0.00	0.00
Billing system		Section IV, subsection J, q.2-3	0.00	0.00	0.00
eDiscovery solutions		Section IV, subsection F, q.1-16	0.00	0.00	0.00
Diversity	**10%**		0.00	0.00	0.00
Firm demographics		Section III, subsection D, q.1&2	0.00	0.00	0.00
Development program		Section III, subsection D, q.3	0.00	0.00	0.00
	100%				

Figure 1: An example of a scorecard used by procurement to evaluate proposals

Strategies to remember

1. Look at the RPF from the client's perspective;
2. Follow instructions carefully – double check all mandatory requirements;
3. Use the selection criteria as a checklist; and
4. Have someone not on the proposal team review the proposal.

Chapter 4:
Working strategically as a team

Everyone knows that when the proposal team and the lawyers work well together, the proposal will be the best it can be, so what's the problem? Answer: each group has their own perspective and role. I find that the kick-off meeting is a good time to outline the roles and expectations of the proposal manager and the lawyers. I don't intend to outline all the steps in a proposal process in this book because while there are common milestones, each firm's structure requires a customized approach. Chapter 6 goes into more detail about the kick-off meeting. In this chapter, I would like to discuss how the proposal manager should work with lawyers and subject matter experts (SMEs) and how lawyers and SMEs can work with the proposal manager. Without cooperation between these disparate groups the proposal process will not go well and instead of it being a strategic exercise it could turn out to be a very frustrating experience. Let me say that I strongly believe that there needs to be respect for each one's role to enable cooperation.

It is important for the proposal manager to build a good relationship with partners and SMEs during the proposal process. The partners need to be able to work from a framework of trust. Therefore, no typos in drafts is a good place to start. Being prepared for meetings is another Demonstrating an understanding of the business is another big one. The same applies when working with SMEs who have clear-cut roles. They need you to give them as much advance notice as possible for them to provide you with their input.

In most cases, you will be treated as professionally as you project yourself. The role of proposal managers varies depending upon the structure of the proposal function at the firm. Below is the typical role of the proposal manager.

The role of the proposal manager/team

Basically, the proposal manager has overall accountability for the proposal process. This includes liaising with the management team, lead lawyer(s), proposal team lawyers, SMEs, production department and delivery department. The manager will ensure that the right internal support is available when needed.

The proposal manager is in charge of the proposal core team and develops the proposal plan, ensures the proposal is compliant, and has woven the win themes into the document. If the manager has a team, the following tasks will be divvied up between various team members:

- Initiates go/no-go decision with lead partner;
- Analyses RFP;
- Develops proposal outline;
- Creates timeline schedule;
- Records the mandatory requirements;
- Organizes the kick-off meeting;
- Works with lawyers on bid strategy;
- Engages SMEs for content;
- Monitors progress of the proposal and maintains proposal schedule;
- Directs writing/editing/rewriting efforts;
- Organizes team for final review and internal evaluation of the proposal;
- Assigns proof-reader;
- Arranges for production; and
- Ensures the proposal is delivered on time.

From a proposal manager's perspective, they are concerned about hitting deadlines, getting the best information from the lawyers and SMEs, and ensuring winning strategies are in the bid document.

It is important to be very clear as to the information you are asking the lawyers to provide. I remember a proposal team manager asking a partner to provide information for a proposal. He thought it was clear as to what information he needed. The partner spent all weekend writing pages and pages of great information – the only problem was that he only needed a few paragraphs. Needless to say, the partner was not pleased and it took quite some time for the proposal manager to regain the trust of the partner.

I find it helpful to let the partner know that bullets are fine and that I will put the information into sentences for approval. Provide the lawyer and SME with an outline of the information you need. Here is a list of "To dos" when requesting information:

- Attach the RFP and selection criteria to an email;
- Highlight information requested;
- Provide an outline of the required information;
- Provide win themes;
- Send boilerplate that can be edited;
- Ask for any differentiators that can be added to the proposal;
- State how much information is needed e.g. half a page, a paragraph;
- Let the lawyer know the deadline for the response; and
- Send timeline (workback) schedule.

Working with the proposal manager

When I facilitate my proposal workshop I ask the attendees what their biggest challenges are working with proposal managers and working with lawyers. The number one issue for the proposal manager is the lawyer or SME not delivering the information on time. This often creates a domino effect or a chain reaction that takes the proposal off track. There is not a single person working for a law firm who does not know that clients come first (because they'd be "dehired" if they didn't). It is therefore critical for lawyers to let the proposal manager know in advance if the timeline given for information to be delivered is not possible to meet. It is always a good idea to assign a backup partner who can provide information in lieu of the partner on the proposal team, particularly if the lawyer is a litigator.

Another very common response is that significant changes are made at the last minute, driving the proposal close to being late. One time I asked a lawyer why, when I work with engineers I finish the proposal a day ahead of time whereas, when I am working with lawyers they push the timeline to the limit. Here is the explanation and in an unsettling way it makes sense. In effect he said:

"Engineers work with processes and follow strict guidelines as to how to undertake a project. Lawyers, on the other hand, can change their approach so they are never really done writing about what they can do for a client; plus they are wordsmiths so they just can't leave the document alone."

This may be an oversimplification, but I understand what he meant. The only thing I can say is that a good artist knows when to put down the brush. A perfectly written late proposal still loses.

I asked several senior procurement people when they'd like to see a proposal delivered. They all said a day in advance because that gives them a clear indication of what kind of a law firm they are dealing with and what they can expect from them in the way of timely service. Feel free to use this insight with your lawyers and SMEs. The client definitely ties the RFP experience back to what kind of service they can expect from your law firm.

Many proposal managers have expressed having a comfort level when they are familiar with the industry and lawyers on particular teams. That is no surprise, but perhaps it would be good for the lawyer to spend a little time bringing the uninitiated up to speed on the industry and why the practice areas requested in the RFP are relevant. Anyone can appreciate how difficult it would be to be thrown into a proposal where you don't know any of the lawyers or issues of the client. It only takes a few minutes and the end result is worth it.

It is helpful when lawyers suggest proposals that they have recently worked on similar to the RFP at hand. It can give the team a starting point. The only problem with this approach is that the lawyer may want the content to be a carbon copy of the last proposal. Everything has to be customized to the client's needs. Depending upon the timeframe it is sometimes a good thing to start with a blank sheet as it encourages "thinking outside the box".

The role of lawyers

Proposals need a lead partner. This is generally the client relationship partner. As an exercise in my proposal workshop, we analyze an RFP and the corresponding proposal. One occasion when I read the proposal supplied by a client for the exercise I thought that they must have won the bid. And I was correct. It was right on point, no "marketing speak," it was clear and concise; they did everything right. We discussed a few things that they could consider in the future but overall the proposal was well done. The proposal manager said that the proposal was challenging because the partner had a definite approach as to how he wanted to present the information. He did not want any "marketing speak"; it had to be concise and all the information had to be relevant. He knew his client and what the client wanted. Later, under other circumstances, I met the general counsel of the company that they had proposed to and I agreed completely with his assessment.

As much as proposal strategists would like to think that we win proposals, it is actually the lawyers who work with us who win the proposals. We can put together a great sounding document but we need the lawyers' input all the way along. They are the ones who understand the client's style, understand their needs and how they can solve their problems. They know the pricing that will be acceptable, how to differentiate the firm's offering, and verify the strategies that will work. We need great input from them. We are the guides. They are the providers. They have the information buried deep inside themselves; our role is to get it out of their mind and put it on paper. I didn't say it was easy, but it is critical.

We also need lawyers to trust us when we present a good case for including or not including information in a tender. We have a storehouse of information and expertise that we have gathered from working on sometimes hundreds of proposals. We have seen what works and what does not work. We have also conducted many debriefs about what clients like and don't like about bids and are committed to bring it to the table. In the end, it is the lead partner who will make the final decision. I have found that the more committed the lead partner is, the higher the probability of winning.

The role of the lead partner includes, but is not limited, to the following tasks:

- Determines go/no-go decision;
- Meets with proposal manager prior to team meeting;
- Leads or co-leads the kick-off meeting;
- Works with the proposal manager to ensure the proposal is on track;
- Becomes escalation contact for late input;
- Reviews drafts to ensure strategy is evident;
- Leads pricing discussions;
- Prepares red team review with the proposal manager; and
- Submits proposal in his/her name.

Working with lawyers

As I mentioned earlier, when I facilitate my workshop I ask the attendees what their biggest challenges are working with lawyers or the proposal manager. Lawyers also have their pet peeves. A common complaint is that the proposal manager is not well prepared for meetings and wastes the lawyer's time. Prepare your questions or concerns before your meeting and have the documents you want to discuss ready.

Another barrier to not working well with lawyers can be not understanding how each lawyer works. Each lawyer and has his/her own style and preferences. As a consultant and constantly working with different partners within largely differing cultures, I find that legal assistants are invaluable in helping me work well with lawyers from day one. Some lawyers like to communicate via email, others prefer a quick face-to-face meeting or brief phone call. Others don't want to hear from you directly and prefer everything be sent through their assistant.

The following example is looking at things from a different perspective. I was working with a lawyer on a bid that had to be done the next day. At noon on the first day, I sent him a rough draft asking if I was on the right track as he had been out of the office. He came running to my office and said, "Nancey, you put the present and past tense as the first word for the bullets – 'acted' and 'acting'." I said, "Yes, some matters are in process and others have been completed". He said, "I can't get past the grammar, I have found another way of wording the matters so this doesn't happen. I can't see the big picture when I see these little things." Actually, I completely sympathized with him as I have the same problem. Later, I looked up his bio and saw that he had an English major in his undergraduate degree. Had I checked it earlier I would have waited and sent a proofread draft so he could have focused on the big picture. Our perspective was different. In my mind, time was of the essence; in his mind, it was grammar.

Lawyers understand that you are not a lawyer but they do expect you to understand the services they offer to some degree. Some basic knowledge goes a long way. For example, if you are dealing with a Canadian client on an employment and labor issue you would want to know if the client is unionized or non-unionized, public or private, provincial or federal. That way you will know what matters to pull together for the proposal. One firm where I worked had the lead partner of various practice groups speak with the proposal and business development teams about their practice area. It was great to see the enthusiasm of the lawyers when they described what they did for a living and the information was invaluable. I credit those sessions for helping me beyond measure when I am working with various practice groups. I highly recommend that other firms adopt this kind of information session.

I am sure lawyers could go on about how they would like the proposal manager to work with them. It would be a good idea for the proposal manager to speak with the lawyers in advance to determine their style and expectations.

Here is a list of "To dos:"

- Find out how the lawyer would like to work with you;
- Prepare for meetings, no matter how informal;
- Be organized: plan ahead, set agendas, take good notes, send follow-up memos;
- Respond to your lawyer's questions with direct and detailed answers;
- If you do not understand, ask questions until you fully understand; and
- Keep lawyers informed regarding the status of the proposal.

The role of subject matter experts

The role of subject matter experts means different things to different firms. Working with subject matter experts (SMEs) including knowledge management (KM), legal project management (LPM), information security (IS), and pricing is an important part of the proposal process. No matter what the specific role of the SME, they fulfill some basic tasks:

- Deliver specific client-centric information;
- Identify differentiators;
- Provide pricing information;
- Explain processes;
- Supply input about the firm's technology;
- Describe approaches and provide technical details;
- Authenticate the content; and
- Confirm that the solution can be implemented.

Working with subject matter experts

When working with SMEs I find that asking them to write bullets and not necessarily full sentences gets me the information faster. Then I put the information into the needed format and send it back for verification.

Here are some additional tips:

- Send the section of the RFP that applies to them, or the entire RFP with the section highlighted;
- Provide an outline of the information you need and the length of response required;
- Highlight the selection criteria that applies to their input;
- Offer boilerplate if available and how you need it to be edited; and
- Provide deadline for when information is due.

Knowledge management

Knowledge management (KM) can be quite diverse and often overlaps with IT. Knowledge managers support pricing, process improvement, and legal project management. Their role is to put into place standard procedures to support a more efficient and effective operation of the law firm. Some of their duties include developing centralized repositories of precedents, legal opinions, and case studies. Selected tasks are itemized below.

Role of knowledge managers

- Create innovative legal products and tools to address specific business needs;
- Implement collaboration platforms;
- Develop a portal strategy;
- Initiate data mining strategies; and
- Leverage technology to control legal costs.

Legal project management

Most RFPs ask how the firm manages matters. Today, clients want details on how their projects will be run. Legal project managers scope projects and provide a comfort level for clients on how their matters will be managed as well as information on which the pricing team bases their calculations.

Role of legal project managers

Legal project managers are regarded as essential to the delivery of consistent, well-organized and cost-effective legal services so they also work with pricing, knowledge management, and IT teams. They are an integral part of the team because when projects are properly scoped it decreases the number of write-offs, thus making the firm more profitable. They typically have a close relationship with clients and track client satisfaction on the delivery of services and, when necessary, identify any changes that need to be made

Their role includes:

- Ensure matters are properly scoped from the outset;
- Verify matters are appropriately budgeted;
- Review staffing models; and
- Monitor matters closely throughout the engagement – both the process and budget.

Proposal management strategies

This book focuses on the role strategy plays at every step of the proposal process. Much of the time spent on a proposal is spent gathering relevant information and strategizing what it will take to win. So what does all this information about working with SMEs have to do with strategy?

RFPs are asking more detailed questions about how projects are managed and what innovations your firm has developed to be more efficient. Both LPM and KM can give you a competitive edge when crafting responses regarding matter management and innovative technology initiatives.

Legal project management enables law firms to practice what they preach when it comes to managing matters, improving efficiency, and saving costs. Knowledge management improves service delivery as they support legal project management and provide avenues for process improvement and provide current technical solutions to the firm and clients.

Strategies to remember

1. Define the roles of the proposal team at the beginning of the bid process to build a good working relationship;
2. Provide clear instructions for the kind of information required; and
3. Understand the roles of the SMEs to get their best input.

Chapter 5: Doing your homework to identify strategies

The purpose of this chapter is not to have an in-depth discussion on how big data and artificial intelligence are transforming law and the legal profession – that is a book unto itself – but rather we will look at various research methods and sources of information that can give you a strategic advantage. In addition, you will understand what kind of tools in-house counsel is using to measure the performance of their legal services providers.

Today, law firms and their clients are engaging in data mining activities to a growing degree and new software is being developed at a startling pace. In fact, it is now being referred to as "deep learning". Technology is being used to determine profitable and competitive pricing models, perform cost analysis, map out process improvements, plan legal project management activities, and measure law firm effectiveness.

LexisNexis and Westlaw Legal are two data-driven research entities that function primarily as huge search engines. These companies have databases containing huge amounts of case details by region and are often the starting point for legal librarians and researchers. Law firms can research their competition by monitoring competitive intelligence databases that are both lawful and legal. For openers, information can be accessed on legal work being done by a prospect or client and data can be utilized to analyze opposing counsel.

A growing number of in-house legal departments are using internal information and market data to determine pricing predictability. They have a wealth of information about competitive pricing and can do their own analysis. One method they use is to request hourly rates and perform their own calculations as to where a quote or range of costs for a matter should be. When analyzing AFAs, they need to know how the AFAs are scoped in order to do their own math. To be strategic when pricing matters, law firms need to be transparent in their pricing to gain credibility with their clients. Proposals present a great opportunity to prove that you are competitive and fair in your pricing.

I recently spoke at a conference on the topic of pricing to in-house and external legal practitioners on the benefits of leveraging client service teams and analyzing the profitability of various staffing models. When I asked for a show of hands to see who was in the audience, the majority of the attendees were in-house counsel. It just goes to show that there is great interest amongst in-house lawyers about how pricing scenarios are developed by law firms. Add to your proposal strategy information on how you price your AFAs.

If you don't know the purchasers of your legal services, how can you sell to them? I have broken this section into two parts. Internal research meaning the information about the client that is available through the law firm's internal data sources. External research meaning the information that you would research by using an external information source, for example, commercial databases, the internet, and libraries.

Internal research

Law firms possess massive amounts of potentially useful data that often goes untapped. Lawyers can mine their client data to predict what matters cost in the past based on experience with a certain type of matter, geography, industry, complexity, and service team. Knowledge management specialists are being hired to analyze information that is buried in finance and IT. Some firms have developed their own databases while others purchase software to analyze their client activity. This includes:

Historical information:

- Client;
- Service teams;
- Services;
- Industry;
- Matters;
- Pricing;
- AFAs;
- Billing reports;
- Write-offs;
- Profitability; and
- Who knows who at the company.

Go/no-go bid decision

As part of the go/no-go decision, internal research is essential. I remember an RFP from an existing client for a quick turn-around bid that included several countries. The proposal manager researched the billing history and discovered that the client had not used the firm's services very often in the past three years. Further research showed that nothing within the regulatory arena was happening in the industry in the foreseeable future and the client was not expanding at this time, thus new service offerings would be limited. The opportunity to bid was declined. It takes courage (or should I say strategy?) to turn down a "business opportunity". Was it a true opportunity – or just a case of needing three quotes? I applaud the research that was done to back up this no-go decision.

Previous proposals

Proposals that were submitted to the client for previous bids are a valuable source of information. It is a good idea to review past scoping and pricing arrangements and validate how you lived up to your commitments. If you promised to conduct monthly meetings, include actions that were undertaken in your next proposal or performance review.

Proposal debrief

Hopefully you have a copy of the proposal debrief as to why you won or lost. Now you know the areas where you provided good information and where you need to improve your next proposal. I always recommend a debrief whether you win or lose a bid. Remember, particularly for public sector bids, you will need to re-propose when the contract ends, so gaining insight directly from the buyer is beneficial going forward. I have received valuable feedback that I catalog for future use following win/lose debriefs.

Client satisfaction reviews

Another great source of information is obtained from client satisfaction reviews. Surveys or in-person reviews are an excellent way to gain insightful information for bids. It is better to know when there is an issue rather than losing a client because something has not been dealt with to the client's satisfaction. Time and again, client satisfaction reviews are not followed up. What a wasted opportunity. Not only that, but if grievances are not fixed immediately, it is worse than not conducting a client satisfaction review in the first place. A strategic plan is important to develop once you have the feedback from your client. This is all good fodder for proposals. You can include actions you took to remedy a situation showing your response to client feedback. Put this information in your proposal under "listening and acting on your feedback".

Client meetings

Closely related to client satisfaction reviews are regular meetings held with the client. The proposal team needs access to the notes from these meetings, particularly if there is not a client service team assigned to the client. These meetings typically focus on how to improve service delivery, processes, efficiency, industry trends, cross-selling, and legal strategies. In the article, "Shell Oil on relieving pressure on corporate legal departments,"[1] Christopher Jeffery, Thomson Reuters market development lead for legal, interviewed Vincent Cordo, Royal Dutch Shell's global sourcing officer, about the role of panel firms. Cordo stated that:

> *"Our panel of relationship partners communicate regularly with our general counsel and business leaders. They have quarterly meetings to review activities in the industry and key facts in a one-on-one forum to discuss strategy and our relationship."*

Again, great material for your proposal.

Client service team meeting minutes

Check your internal client service team meeting minutes. Many law firms have client service teams assigned to manage key clients. The teams are comprised of the lead partner, practice area partners, industry lead partners, and often client managers and business development managers. Key client meetings provide a forum to understand your client's goals, strategies, issues, problems, operations, systems, reporting requirements, processes, preferred working method, and corporate culture. This is all valuable input for proposal teams. Because information is exchanged among lawyers servicing the client about trends and developments affecting their client's business and within their industry, the proposal team can flip this information into great content.

Client performance meetings

Performance meetings offer an opportunity for the client to engage in an open conversation with outside counsel and let them know where they stand relative to their competition. The competitive information gained at these meetings is very beneficial for the proposal team. Clients depend on information law firms know about their industry. In the same article quoted above, Cordo commented that:

> *"Paying attention to factors such as economics, industry shifts, technology developments and other influences that may impact our business is key. For example, in the regulatory environment, nothing happens overnight. You need to be strategic when planning and not rely only on your internal expertise. We work with external vendors to get their perspective on what they see. We regularly engage our legal panel to gauge the impact of trends and what's on the horizon in our industry."*

Meeting minutes provide invaluable information on how to strategize your proposal. It is a treasure trove of evidence that demonstrates that you really understand your client's business and the industry.

Key performance indicators

In this instance, when I talk about Key Performance Indicators (KPIs) I mean the KPIs that are put forth by the client. Not the KPIs that are formulated by law firms that reflect their service delivery goals. Many lawyers are surprised to learn that their more sophisticated clients have over 100 KPIs that they use to measure law firm and individual lawyer performance. Ask your client about the KPIs they use to measure your service deliverables and work them into your KPIs and proposal content.

Corporations focus on scoring performance as it relates to matter results and pricing. However, other important KPIs that are measured are an understanding about the company's priorities, business goals, industry knowledge, efficiency, responsiveness, process management, responsiveness, and budgeting

Additional client KPIs:

- Results delivered, rate of success;
- Actual spending vs budgeted spending;
- Comparative fees between competitors;
- Timely submission of reports; and
- Types of AFAs provided.

Diversity and inclusion

This is a growing need for companies that wish to be taken seriously. Not only are companies being rated on their diversity, they are also being rated on the diversity of their vendors, including law firms. Many corporations have made commitments regarding their position on diversity and inclusion public on their website and vow to live up to their promises.

Some countries do not presently require companies to record or publish statistics on diversity and inclusion, let alone report them in proposals. However, as many RFPs are sent by countries where diversity and inclusion statistics are mandatory, it would be a good tactic to present your statistics and policies in proposals, even if not required to do so.

Knowing your numbers

Researching your financial information is a good place to start when analyzing fees and processes for robust proposal content. Law firms should analyze:

- Billings;
- Budget reports, showing line items by activity;
- Reports showing the number of new matters opened, existing matters, and closed matters; and
- Reports showing the amount of fees and expenses incurred for matters.

Below are some templates for reports that can be customized to reflect data that is accessible from internal sources that can be used as a guide for internal proposal research.

Client name:			
AFA description	**Introduced**	**Fee**	**Profitability**

Figure 5.1: Alternative fee arrangements report

Client name	Matter/ project name	Lead partner	Industry	Practice area	Country

Figure 5.2: Matter summary report

Matter	Fees year-to-date	Profitability	Office	Year
Practice area				
Industry				
Total				

Figure 5.3: Matter report

External research

When I was a researcher for a Top Four management consulting firm, I was amazed about the amount of information that was publicly available – and that was before the internet. I went to university business libraries and searched for information in hardbound business articles indexes and government documents. It was hard work, but it taught me how to know when I hit pay dirt; for example, when I saw the same article show up in different indexes by using different search terms I knew I'd found the article I was looking for. That experience has helped me when I use electronic systems to research information on a client or industry.

Before data mining, many decisions were based on personal experience. If a lawyer won in front of a particular judge he/she thought they could easily win again. Now lawyers can research cases, lawyers, judges, and the outcome of a matter to determine the probability of success.

Today, law firms are starting to follow their clients by creating systems or utilizing data analyzing tools for a full range of uses such as to predict the damages that might be awarded in a particular case or analyze data to identify candidates that will fit into their firm's culture.

Lawyers are often surprised when I explain how their clients are using technology to analyze competitive rates and performance down to the individual lawyer level. Data analysis allows in-house legal departments to predict pricing scenarios for various bids. Many law firms are now using analytics to benchmark themselves against the industry and use commercially available data sources to compare their rates against the competition.

All of the above research methods and sources of information can put you in a strong competitive position and proposal strategies will stem from this data. It is critical that you do your homework for each proposal opportunity. Research is key to determining winning strategies. Make sure you have all the facts and figures.

Whether or not you are the incumbent, ask yourself the following questions:

- What do we know about the company?
- Who do we think will influence the decision?
- What do we know about the industry?
- What do we know about the competition?
- What differentiates us from the competition?
- What information do have internally that will support our strategy?
- Do we have the expertise and work cycles?

Larger law firms have libraries and research librarians on staff who have access to numerous databases such as Bloomberg and LexisNexis. If your law firm does not have this facility in-house you can use the internet and access commercial databases.

Kinds of information to research:

- Company website;
- Annual reports;
- Executives;
- Board members;
- Organizational structure;
- Corporate strategy and goals;
- Mission statement;
- Company values;
- Company charities;
- Industry websites;
- Government agencies;
- Industry databases;
- Legal databases;
- Market analysis reports;
- News articles;
- Big deals;
- League tables, and
- Legal directories.

Competitive intelligence

Zena Applebaum, corporate strategy, competitive intelligence for the legal industry, says:

> *"Competitive intelligence is key for determining differentiation. Research your past deals and perform deal analytics. Look at who was on the deal and reflect that with the team you are putting forward in your proposal.*
>
> *"Research company/prospects to see if they have a policy of hiring 50 percent females for their executive committee, or some other kind*

of diversity initiative, and then make sure your proposed team reflect a similar position. Matching and mirroring the culture of your clients is key to building trust.

"Competitive intelligence is not just for the moment but looking forward, for example, continue to research the company following the submission of your bid to keep on top of what is happening at the company. It is great when you can mention a recent press release at a verbal presentation to demonstrate your current knowledge of the company."

Develop a corporate profile to get a snapshot of the company or prospect to identify missing information and get a clear picture of the opportunity.

Company name	
Executives	
Board members	
General counsel	
In-house counsel	
Industry	
Industry issues/trends	
Total revenue	
Country where head office resides	

Client type (tick all applicable)

- Local
- National
- International

Description of business

Firm's contacts at company ("who knows who")

Figure 5.4: Corporate profile

Strategies to remember

1. Internal research can be used to document the great service you provide your clients;
2. External research supports your knowledge about the client and their industry;
3. Competitive intelligence can give you an advantage when mapping out your strategies; and
4. In-house counsel is tracking the same kind of information law firms are tracking on KPIs; make sure you are in sync.

Reference

1. https://blogs.thomsonreuters.com/answerson/shell-oil-relieving-pressure-on-corporate-legal-departments/

Chapter 6:
Kick-off meeting strategies

Before the kick-off meeting

I strongly believe that the kick-off meeting is critical to the success of a proposal. This is when you get the rare opportunity to have all the key players in the same room at the same time. It is at this meeting that the strategies percolate. It is undoubtedly my favorite part of the proposal process. Unfortunately, it is often a step that is not taken due to busy schedules. I recommend scheduling a short kick-off meeting rather than not having one at all.

I understand that small bids do not require a formal kick-off meeting. However, I am still suggesting that a brief team discussion take place to decide on the strategies. Lead practice area partners or industry partners can recommend strategies that may not have been otherwise considered. Even if you just send the RFP to a knowledgeable partner for his/her point of view it is better than nothing.

Once again I am giving you best practices in a perfect world. The following information is for a "perfect" kick-off meeting.

An important early step is to issue an RFP notification for all large bids to all lawyers in the firm. If you belong to a global firm you will need to decide which countries/offices should get the bid notification. Finding out who knows who is important when formulating teams and collecting intelligence. It is amazing who knows the client, has done work for the client while working at another firm, knows something relevant in the industry, or has written a book. One time a client was looking for a lawyer with a special kind of expertise and we found out that a new hire had written a book on that very subject. He was obviously added to the team.

Figure 6.1 overleaf is a sample of an RFP notification that can be modified for your use.

RFP notification	
Client/company name:	
Client contact name:	
Description of client/company	
Lead partner	
Key partners	
Lead office	
Opportunity	
Reason for bidding	
Key objective(s) of RFP	
Existing client	Yes/No Provide details if appropriate
Industry sector(s) affected	

Practice area(s) requested
Location(s) requested
Who knows who?
Proposal manager
Pricing manager
Legal project management manager
Date: Kick-off meeting
Date: Deadline for submission

Figure 6.1: Sample RFP notification form

Sometimes in order to get the proposal moving, the kick-off meeting is scheduled too soon, before important information is gathered. In a perfect world all the relevant information would be sent to the proposal team partners in advance and reviewed by everyone. This rarely happens. I recommend keeping the pre-meeting reading material as short as possible to encourage the lawyers to look through it. The better the intelligence gathering before the kick-off meeting, the better the conversations about strategy will be.

Figure 6.2 is a checklist for tasks that should be accomplished before the kick-off meeting if at all possible.

Pre-kick-off meeting checklist		
Task	**Yes**	**No**
Conflicts-of-interest check done including client's terms and conditions if included in the RFP		
Sent "RFP notification" to all lawyers		
Selected and notified key team members		
Sent kick-off meeting agenda to team		
Sent RFP to team, note selection criteria		
Asked team to note questions for clarification		
Compiled information on company		
Compiled information on industry		
Compiled competitor profiles		
If incumbent: Compiled briefing package: client history, billing history, fee history including AFAs and profitability, overall profitability, lawyers who have served the client, mandates, practice areas, offices, successes/losses, client performance reviews, secondments, CLE courses		
Scoped pricing at a high level, identified any issues		

Figure 6.2: Pre-kick-off meeting checklist

The kick-off meeting

You are fortunate if you can book a formal kick-off meeting for an hour of busy lawyers' time. As we know, most of the partners will not have read the RFP and that is why it is imperative that research is done in advance (chapter 5). The lead partner and proposal manager must have reviewed the RFP in detail. Hopefully, much of the homework will have been done prior to the meeting and with a bit of good fortune the lead team members will have already been selected and are present.

Some proposal professionals think that the go/no-go decision should be decided at the kick-off meeting. I disagree. Precious time is wasted discussing the pros and cons of a bid opportunity at the kick-off meeting. Strategy should be your main goal, particularly as it is often difficult to get the whole proposal team together again.

There are many elements making up the strategy of proposals. Here we will discuss pricing, differentiators, team composition, the best experience and expertise that the firm can offer, and value-added services.

Strategy

As I mentioned, my favorite part of the proposal is the kick-off meeting as this is when the strategy comes together. Here is when the proposal team members share their understanding of the client's business and legal issues and decide on win-themes. This is where you hash out why you are the best firm for the engagement.

I love the energy in the room. I love watching the team get enthusiastic and come up with great ideas. I love the commitment towards winning. After all, why else would you spend the time and money proposing? I always say it is not *just* about winning – it is *only* about winning. Using the information gathered in advance will help the team formulate winning tactics. Detailed information on strategies is in Chapter 8 (Strategy: needs, outcomes, solutions, and proof).

Pricing

We all know that pricing is a key component to winning. That is why pricing professionals need to be at the kick-off meeting. If you do not have pricing professionals or a CFO on staff, see if there is a partner who has experience in calculating the best pricing scenarios.

If you are fortunate enough to have pricing professionals at your firm they should have a copy of the RFP. Send them the entire RFP. Sometimes they are just sent the list of team members and what alternative fee arrangements (AFAs) are wanted. That is not getting the best input from pricing professionals, who work on bids all day long. They can discuss strategies that have been used for other clients and in other proposals, what will not fly with firm management, and suggest ways to present AFAs. They can confirm the scope and get first-hand information on team members and which offices will be included in the proposal. They can suggest added value options, how processes can be improved, clearly scope the matter, and explain why the pricing scenarios were suggested. This is key to winning. Clients want to understand how you came up with the price. Basically, they want price transparency.

I am not going to discuss pricing in this book as it has been written about in great detail by many knowledgeable authors. I recommend that you read *Smarter Profit, Smarter Pricing* and *Pricing on the Front Line*, both by Stuart Dodds, published by the American Bar Association. Stuart is the co-founder/principal of Positive Pricing, and former director of global pricing and legal project management at Baker McKenzie.

Key differentiators

Chapter 9 is devoted to differentiation but it goes without saying that differentiators are critical to the success of any proposal. I have written proposals for many law firms and I can tell you that law firms can look very similar. Firms need to differentiate themselves. Years ago, I would have said that it was not easy to differentiate one firm from another. However, today with technology, artificial intelligence, cybersecurity, outsourcing, legal project management, to name a few, it is much easier to distinguish your firm. I find that relevant differentiators come out of these meetings because they are customized for a particular proposal.

Team composition

The client usually itemizes the kind of experience and expertise they are looking for. Team selection should be thought about carefully from the beginning. I know that it is not always possible to select all the team members in the initial meeting, particularly if the proposal requires more than one office or country. However, serious thought should go into selecting the right team member at the right price as soon as possible. Inevitability, some team members will get changed as the partners start working on the proposal. Nevertheless, once you start changing team members the domino effect takes place. New team members have to drop everything to get on board, dropped team members are not happy about wasting their time on the bid, the proposal team hurries to get bios customized, the pricing team rushes to change the pricing, and sometimes senior management must be contacted at the last minute for new budget approval.

It is increasingly important that associates, pricing professionals, and legal project managers are included in the mix. When I have conducted proposal debriefings this issue often comes up. Clients get nervous when they see too many partners and no associates assigned to a matter. When you show the levels of associates on your team and then say the work will be assigned to the most appropriate level, your statement becomes believable. This is backed up in the pricing section when you show a full range of pricing by using associates. Proposals have been lost because they were too partner-heavy without providing a good reason why.

If a verbal presentation is required, it is important from the outset to select lawyers who will make a good impression. This may make the team selection more difficult, but it will pay off when you present to the client.

Just because a particular partner receives the RFP it doesn't necessarily mean that he/she should be the lead partner. I remember an occasion where the RFP was sent to an employment and labor partner as there was a previous connection; however, the work was primarily for environmental work. I discussed this situation with the partner and suggested that an environment partner co-sign the covering letter so that it was clear that we understood that the primary mandate of the RFP was environmental. It was done and due to the great team that was put together, we won the bid.

While we are still on the subject of team composition, I would be remiss if I didn't discuss diversity and inclusion. I have had many discussions with procurement and General Counsel about this topic and it is becoming an important issue in the decision-making process as to which firms get hired. All things being equal, the firm with the most diverse team with the necessary qualifications will have a better chance of getting the work. As mentioned previously, many companies are measured on their diversity and the diversity of their suppliers. I think you would be surprised to hear some of the conversations I have had on this topic. If you don't believe me, feel free to discuss it with your client.

At the meeting, confirm content that will come from each team member so that the "tasks/timelines schedule" will be as complete as possible when circulating the schedule to the team following the kick-off meeting.

Last but not least, make sure the proposal manager has a back-up partner who can respond to questions if a lead partner is away, and should there be a presentation, make sure all key members of the team will be available. I have seen it happen that the presentation takes place when a key partner is out of the country. This does not bode well with the client. Even if another senior partner steps in to emphasize the importance of the client to the firm, it seems to fall flat.

I have spent time discussing the team at kick-off meetings because I always say that you get your foot in the door because of the firm's well-earned reputation, but you win bids because of your team. Every general counsel and procurement professional that I have spoken with says that they hire the people with the best expertise and price comes in second to that.

Mandates

If there are any mandates that differentiate your firm and team members, they should be mentioned at the meeting. These should show up in the proposal and bios of the team members. Mandates are the proof that you have done the type of work before and been successful. Don't leave it entirely up to the proposal manager to decide which mandates are the best to include in the bid. Let them know the best ones that elevate your profile above that of the competition.

Selection criteria

Remember that the selection criteria are a gift, especially if they give you the weightings. These should be taken to the kick-off meeting to identify strategies. If the RFP has a short turn-around time it will help focus the team's attention on the most important areas where they need to spend time. It will also let you know if it is a fee-driven bid – thus back to strategy.

Weaknesses and gaps

The RFP and selection criteria will help you identify any weaknesses or gaps that you may have in responding to the RFP. Hopefully these have been discussed during the go/no-go decision and you can spend time at the meeting to mitigate your shortcomings. If you can't prove that you are the best firm, you should back out and save your reputation for a better opportunity.

Added value services

The kick-off meeting is a good time to discuss meaningful added value services. Some suggestions may require the approval of senior management, e.g. secondments and pricing discounts. It is timely to have these discussions early on so as to get approval before going too far down the line.

Questions for clarification

It is good to discuss questions for clarification at the kick-off meeting as some questions can be tricky because you don't want to give away your strategies and if you are the incumbent you don't want to divulge any useful information to the competition. This is when you need a group think. Some firms don't send any questions and wait to see what the competition is asking. However, many of the procurement people I know appreciate the questions that come in as it is perceived as an indication that the RFP is taken seriously and certain firms are asking insightful questions.

I recommend that all communication with the client be from the lead partner, not the assistant or the proposal manager as it shows commitment at the highest level. This includes the clarifying questions.

Carefully review the responses to the questions for clarification. These will often reveal competitive information. Sometimes the information is subtle, so it is important to pay close attention to the kinds of questions and how many times the same kind of question was raised and the answers.

I have had the pleasure of running some great kick-off meetings with amazing teams. The teams that I love working with are the teams that want to win. Yes, you heard me right. Sometimes lawyers who have spent a lot of time on proposals and then lost a few bids can become pessimistic and that is understandable. But it is a fact of life: you win some, you lose some. It is important to come with your game face on. If you have the qualifications and the right pricing, why shouldn't you win? It is enthusiastic teams that put forth the best bids. Ask partners who are not going to be on the team but have great ideas to join the meeting. I remember one kick-off meeting where a partner was known for his out-of-the-box thinking. He was only asked to attend the kick-off meeting, but he added great value to the proposal. I also remember a managing partner who attended all kick-off meetings for large bids. This partner was very strategic and knew everyone in the firm and the competition. I would ask him what firms he thought we'd be competing against and what lawyers at those firms were most likely to be on the opposing team and he'd provide me with a list of names. I'd then research the firms and lawyers to make sure our proposal was competitive. Needless to say, our win rate was very high.

After the kick-off meeting

Immediately after the kick-off meeting, circulate:

- Kick-off meeting minutes, including win themes, issues to solve/escalate;
- Questions for clarification and ask for additional questions by a specific deadline;
- Bios to each team member to be customized; and
- "Task/timeline schedule" including pricing, knowledge management, IT, and legal project management etc.

Figure 6.3 overleaf is a task/timeline schedule that can be used as a guide to provide information that is needed from each team member and the status of the proposal. It needs to be constantly updated and referred to by the proposal manager. It is a good way tack late information.

Verbal presentations

Rehearsals are a critical component for winning the bid. Your presentation is usually the last step in a long process leading to a win-or-lose decision by the client. If you must choose a lawyer who has the best expertise and experience but is not a good speaker I suggest that you go with the best lawyer for the matter and work with him/her at the rehearsal and privately to help him/her with their presentation skills. In certain cases, I have recommended trainers to coach presenters with good success.

One presentation team that I coached required a consortium of law firms from several countries. The team had never met in person, though we had many discussions over the phone. When they got together for the rehearsal they had great synergy. It was as if they had known each other for years. We were very fortunate. After three rehearsals the team was ready to go. We had discussed the "devil's advocate" questions and responses and they were confident that they could present a rather complex solution to the client. And they did. They were all seasoned partners, but they agreed that without the rehearsals the presentation would have been a disaster (like the first rehearsal). It is not about whether you speak well; most lawyers do. It is a matter of saying the right things and being in sync with the other presenters. I still see partners rushing out to make a presentation without a practice session because they speak for a living. I always say the worst-case scenario is that all the firms have

Client name:								
RFP:								
Proposal section and #	Responsibility	Page/ words limit	Information due date	First draft date/ Feedback date	Second draft date/ feedback date	Final draft date/ sign- off	Status	Delivery date + details

Figure 6.3: Task/timeline schedule

rehearsed their presentation – the best-case scenario is that you have rehearsed and the competition didn't.

The presentation is when the client can see you in action, judge how well you know your information, and how well you interact with the other team members. It gives them an indication of how you would work with them, so it needs to be well prepared.

Kick-off meetings are the first step in setting the strategies that you will build on over the course of preparing your proposal. If you are not in the habit of having kick-off meetings I hope you will implement this process on your next big bid and see the results. You will be amazed.

Strategies to remember

1. Gather intelligence by sending an email to lawyers re: an RFP opportunity;
2. Prepare the team to discuss strategies by distributing well-researched information packages;
3. Take time to select lawyers with the best qualifications early in the bid process; and
4. Think strategy: team, pricing, differentiators, mandates, selection criteria, weaknesses, and added value offerings.

Chapter 7: Different strategies for proposal size and timeline

So far, most of the information contained in this book has been targeted at responding to a formal RFP. However, you are often required to respond to an informal proposal (pitch/credentials). The kind of RFP you are bidding on affects the approach that will be taken. While the same principles apply, you need to scale back your efforts to reply to an informal, short turnaround request. In other words, your proposal processes and content need to be scalable. Some responses may require an email response for a fee quote or a quick credentials package for a particular matter. Formal RFPs, on the other hand, may require a proposal of hundreds of pages.

Whether it is an informal or formal RFP, there is a certain degree of homework that needs to be done, regardless of the type of RFP, even if it is only to speak with the lead partner or industry expert.

Informal pitch/credentials

The packaging of an informal pitch/credential request is as important as a proposal to a formal RFP as it demonstrates your professionalism and creates an immediate impression about your firm. I recently worked on a Public Private Partnership (P3) bid that was on a very tight deadline. Some of the P3 partners said that the look of the document was not very important due to the timeframe. However, we put together a professional looking proposal and the partners agreed that the client's perception of our document would demonstrate our professionalism and keen interest in the project.

The expression, "If I had more time, I would have written a shorter letter" is very true when it comes to proposals. Just because it is a "pitch" doesn't mean it can be done quickly without any forethought. The partner and proposal manager need to focus on key messages/win themes and provide proof as to why you are the right firm to handle the work. I have provided some suggestions under "scalability" on how you can prepare information in advance.

Sometimes informal bids present a list of topics (rather than questions) for which they would like you to present your qualifications. Typical topics include a description of your firm, your proposed team, and your experience and expertise for a list of specific services. Fees are not generally asked for at this stage. It is important to follow the client's format but make sure that you highlight, perhaps using text boxes, your experience and expertise. If you are not asked, you can put your differentiators in a text box too.

Informal (pitch/credentials) project management process:

- Lead partner identified;
- Conflict check request submitted and conflicts cleared;
- Proposal manager meet with lead partner;
- Team identified;
- Services, geography, relevant matters determined;
- Team bios updated;
- Pricing team notified (if required);
- Quick research (company and industry, client background);
- Partner approval for content; and
- Final proposal submitted.

Formal RFP response

The formal RFP is often designed by procurement professionals, many of whom use a software system to analyze responses from the law firms. Other in-house teams analyze content by putting responses on an Excel spreadsheet to compare the answers provided by each law firm. If you have been provided with the selection criteria, this is the time to use it.

A formal proposal requires content from numerous sources across the firm. It also needs a lead partner to work with the team to produce a winning bid. The following is a list of high level questions that need to be asked for a formal RFP response:

- Have you reviewed the RFP for strategies?
- What is the client asking for/what are their needs?
- What information do you need to know?
- What solutions can you offer?

- What benefits can you offer?
- What questions do you need to ask the client for clarification?
- Who should be on the team?
- What SMEs should be involved on the bid (IT, pricing, and legal project manager)?
- What are your win themes?
- What proof can you offer to solidify your proposition?

Scalability

Create a tool kit – desktop, database, or proposal software system – to have ready access to information that can be customized for your proposal/pitch. To start with, content can be put in a MS Word document. Content can be created by extracting copy from past proposals. Taking information from your website should be your last resort. Some schools of thought recommend that you have a list of probable questions and answers. However, I have found that for law firms a template of standard best practices content is the fastest way to put together a shell document. I won't deny that it is a lot of work gathering the content but, in my experience, it is worth the effort.

I would like to add one caveat; if you don't regularly update your standard content it will cease being useful because proposal content is constantly being improved. People will go back to their "C" drive or the last proposal they wrote and reuse the content. This will not give you best practices content to use as a starting point for your proposal.

The key to success is to customize your proposal to meet your client's needs and never just cut and paste generic content. The following best practices content can be created in advance for proposals and pitches:

- General firm information;
- Office descriptions;
- Description of practice areas;
- Description of industry sector expertise;
- Relevant matters by industry/practice area;
- Diversity and inclusiveness policies and statistics;
- Awards/recognition;
- Added value services;

- Biographies (create a long form bio so you can quickly create a short bio); and
- Graphics.

Strategies to remember

1. Informal pitches/credentials need the same professional attention as a formal proposal;
2. Formal RFPs require the full attention of a proposal response team;
3. Selection criteria should be used as your strategic guide; and
4. A tool kit with best practices content is a good starting point.

Chapter 8:
Strategy – needs, solutions, outcomes, and proof

This chapter is where the rubber hits the road. The preceding chapters have led up to this point. If you have been able to undertake the recommendations thus far then many of the elements for this exercise will have already been accomplished. Once again this is best practice in a perfect environment, which we do not often have the luxury to work in. Do what you can, under the time constraints you have been given, and apply strategy to identifying what the client needs, the solutions you can provide, the positive outcomes your solutions will provide, backed up by the proof that you can undertake the work successfully and therefore are the firm to hire.

Needs, solutions, outcomes, and proof are not stand-alone entities – they are all connected. While you may consider each step individually, they must link together in your proposal.

Some RFPs do not specifically state a particular issue that the law firm is expected to solve. Under these circumstances you may think that it is not necessary to analyze needs, solutions, outcomes, and proof as a valid strategic exercise. For example, some RFPs give a laundry list of services they want and ask you to explain your capabilities for each of the practice categories and the team you would propose. Later in this chapter I will show you where you can use this formula – needs, solutions, outcomes, and proof – under those circumstances.

Win themes

Win themes are in essence the key benefits of your offering. By starting with win themes, you establish a strategic outline for your proposal. Win themes should not be written at the end of the proposal process. They are one of the first steps in the proposal process, along with analyzing the RFP and doing your homework (research). Your text will flow from your win themes.

There is no magic number as to how many win themes should be in a proposal. However, less is more in that they should address the needs and reflect the key evaluation points in the selection criteria. Too many themes will get lost in the content. Three to four targeted themes are usually enough.

Position your strengths against the competition's weaknesses and what you think their strategy may be. I have covered competitive research and developing competitor profiles in chapter 5: Doing your homework to identify strategies.

To help you identify win themes, ask the following questions:

- Why have they put out the tender now?
- Do they have legal procurement professionals on staff?
- What are the client's needs/issues?
- What are the client's overall expectations and how can you deliver your services to meet them?
- What benefits and added value are they looking for?
- What evidence can you provide that proves you have the credentials for the engagement?
- Why should the client choose you?

Win themes are always about the client – not you. It is difficult to answer RFP questions that ask about your firm and your credentials and at the same time make it all about the client, but it is possible. Ask yourself:

- Do the win themes demonstrate your understanding of the client's needs/issues?
- Is your solution the best for the situation?
- How much does the result or benefit matter to your client?
- Have you backed up your statements with proof?
- Do the win themes differentiate you from the competition?
- Do the win themes take into consideration the selection criteria?
- Can they be evaluated and scored?

A good exercise you can do with your themes is to delete them from the bid and see whether they made a difference to the persuasion of the proposal. If your win themes are not standing out as to why the client should select your firm, you need to rewrite parts of your document.

Theme statements should focus on the *reasons* you are better than the competition. You need to explain *why* your firm is the best choice. The best win themes tell the client what they will get when they hire you.

Chapter 2, on the go/no-do decision, and chapter 6, on kick-off meeting strategies, provide information that will play into your win themes. The following chart is based on previous chapters of this book, and features some of the questions you can ask to determine your win themes.

Process	Questions to consider
Go/no go decision	What is the state of your relationship with the company? Are you the incumbent? Can you meet the mandatory requirements and terms and conditions? Do you have the qualifications to do the work? Will it be profitable work?
Analyzing the RFP	What are the client's real needs/issues? What is the real scope of work product? What unwritten requirements do they have? How do you exceed the RFP's requirements? How should you position yourself against the evaluation criteria? Have you stressed your strengths and your differentiators? What should you emphasize/deemphasize?
Research client	How well does the client explain their needs? What industry issues may affect the company? Why did the client submit an RFP now?
Research competition	Who is the incumbent? Who are your likely competitors for this bid? How should you position your firm against the competition? What are their strengths/weaknesses compared to your strengths/weaknesses? What pricing considerations should you make?
Strategy	What are the needs, solutions, outcomes, and proof that you are the right choice?

Figure 8.1: Determining win themes

Don't fall into the trap of having all your win themes center on one aspect of what the client needs, such as experience and expertise. Depending on the RFP, themes can be centered on many topics, such as expertise, experience, pricing/AFAs, geography, key performance indicators, process management, efficiencies, and technology.

To keep the content focused on win themes, include theses in emails to partners and SMEs when soliciting their input.

Before analyzing needs, solutions, outcomes, and proof, the following chart gives an overview of how each element is linked.

Needs/issues	• Analyze the needs/issues in the RFP • Use the selection criteria to identify needs and priorities • Consider other issues that are not stated in the RFP • Demonstrate that you understand the client's business and the key needs/issues or needs/issues facing their business and their industry
Solutions	• Actions you are proposing to address their needs/issues – what you are going to do • Recommend solutions that will solve their problems and deliver the desired results
Outcomes/benefits	• Focus on the outcomes/benefits they want to achieve by addressing their needs • Describe favorable outcomes/benefits that will result from the solution you have recommended
Proof	• Support your claim that the solution you have suggested will be effective and that your firm/team has the experience, expertise, and track record to deliver • Provide evidence that you can deliver that your solution on time and on budget • Show that the benefits you have itemized are backed up by proof that you can deliver the outcomes

Figure 8.2: Strategy: needs, solutions, outcomes, proof

Strategies for an existing client

Typically, tenders are for engagements lasting three to five years before going out to bid again. Research shows that incumbents are more likely to win bids if the firm has a good relationship with the client. That being said, legal procurement's role is to be objective when analyzing and recommending law firms. If competitors overshadow the incumbent it could put the incumbent in a negative light and might look like the incumbent has become complacent.

Richard Brzakala, director of external legal services, says:

> *"Firms need to remind themselves that the legal marketplace today is changing at a rapid pace, introducing greater innovation and many different legal service providers who are extremely competitive. Incumbent firms should not assume that their tenure on a panel is indefinite and should leverage any and all inside knowledge for their benefit as outside firms will do any and everything to land a coveted spot on a preferred panel. Firms that have enjoyed the privilege of approved counsel status on a client's panel have a distinct advantage over other firms vying for a similar spot in a competitive RFP bid process."*

Incumbent firms have the benefit of knowing the client and being familiar with internal business processes. If the lawyers have paid attention to their relationship they have a good understanding of the client's budgeting preferences and tolerance for billing limits. This inside information is invaluable and should be leveraged where possible in formulating the incumbent firm's RFP bid strategy.

Procurement is looking for a fresh approach. Sophisticated procurement specialists will review data on the law firm's past performance and the performance of each lawyer. They will also review fees and billings. Therefore, it can be a bit tricky when incumbents offer value-added services in their proposal. The client may wonder why the law firm didn't offer these suggestions before the RFP went out. However, the client expects added value services and better fees, so don't hold back.

The proposal team can get pushback from partners for added value services and better pricing because they believe that they have a great service track record and relationship with the client. That may be so, but as issuing an RFP is a time- consuming process the client wants to leverage their investment and get a better arrangement with the incumbent firm.

If you keep track of the due dates for bid renewals, you will be in a good position to meet with the client in advance of the RFP to determine the client's needs and wants. By knowing the timeframe, you can start preparing your response ahead of the RFP, or better still, pre-empt the need for an RFP (unless it is a private sector client). In either case, keep track of your achievements and successes as they are a great resource for pre-bid conversations and re-bids.

Achievements include your history with the client, how difficult situations were handled, fee quotes that were on target, projects delivered on time or early, track record of success, knowledge of their business and industry, continuous improvement initiatives, and client performance measurement feedback.

Needs/issues

Some companies state specific issues/needs upfront in the RFP, such as reducing legal costs, increasing their global footprint, improving efficiency of legal services, reducing risk, setting up a new entity, and the list goes on. These are easier RFPs to respond to as the client has clearly stated their objectives. That is not to say that you don't have to read between the lines to identify their needs/issues and discuss what they may require along the way to meeting their goals. Other RFPs are not as clear as to the reason why they have gone out for bid and this will require research on your part. Sometimes RFPs are issued to get a sense of how a law firm could solve their problem but aren't specific because they don't want to expose their true corporate issues openly.

Value propositions focus on issues/needs. The section of the proposal on needs is an opportunity for you to show your understanding of your client's needs or issues. You should propose what you can do to enhance their business goals. It may include such issues as needing to enhance their business processes to improve efficiencies, save money, minimize risk, and improve operations or global legal communications. Ensure you identify the correct needs as this drives the overall strategy.

There are many books in the marketplace that talk about client levels of pain, pain points or pain chains or ask, "What keeps you up at night?" It all boils down to identifying the issues of the c-suite and how their pain can cascade through the company, the impact of those pains on other departments in the organization is your opportunity to solve the painful issues/problems. When identifying needs/issues, give consideration as to what pain points your client is having or will have and show how you can solve them. This shows that you understand the client and the legal issues that will be involved.

Analyzing needs, solutions, outcomes, and proof is a linear process; however, sometimes, I find that it is good to brainstorm strategies by analyzing the information by first looking at things from the client's perspective then from the standpoint of the firm. By starting with client needs/issues and then outcomes/benefits you focus solely on the client. Afterwards, consider solutions the firm will provide and proof/evidence that you have the right credentials. Figure 8.3 shows how this process is carried out.

Client	
Needs/issues	You are concerned with legal issues concerning diversity and inclusion (D&I) and want to broaden the skills of your in-house legal team regarding this. You also want to ensure that you are compliant with government regulations.
Outcome/benefits	Our clients have expressed that they have more confidence in handling D&I issues.
Your firm	
Solutions	We offer courses on the social and legal implications of D&I in the workplace at no cost to our clients. We offer seminars to support human resources managers at no cost. We can also assist your in-house legal department and human resources department with up-to-date newsletters on D&I employment issues. Our website has regular blogs, webinars, and brochures featuring current legal issues on D&I.
Proof/evidence	Recently, we won a major D&I case for our client involving wrongful dismissal (describe relevant matter). We would be happy to refer you to our clients who have taken advantage of our courses on D&I issues. Recent topics that may interest you are: • Recent changes to legislation regarding D&I for in-house counsel; and • Human resources hiring issues that include D&I.

Figure 8.3: The client's needs and issues.

Whatever process you choose, by taking the time to brainstorm needs, solutions, outcomes, and proof you will come up with strategies that will relate to your win themes and your entire proposal will hang together. Unfortunately, there are no shortcuts.

Solutions

Solutions are an essential part of your proposal, so it is important not to just list features but rather discuss the impacts or benefits of your solution. The solutions you provide must relate back to the needs or the specific situation your client faces.

To address the issue, formulate solutions by writing a general statement about your recommendation, then narrow down your scope to what your solution will do for your client, for example, how a software program will work to their benefit. Address each need and provide a solution for each. Lastly, provide proof.

Your solutions will confirm your understanding of the needs/issues and the reason why your approach will not result in the problems that other approaches might have. Solutions provide a platform on which to demonstrate your expertise and why the client should choose your firm.

Your solutions link back to your client's needs and, as I explained earlier, you need to show the linkage between the needs and solution, benefit and proof. You could use the layout described in Figure 8.4 as a guide.

Outcomes/benefits

While solutions relate to needs/issues, outcomes relate to solutions and your value propositions. Your solution can be a deal breaker if it is not seen as a benefit to the client and if your promise is not backed up by evidence.

To establish your value proposition first, you need to know which benefits would mean the most to your client. Next, you need to quantify the benefits. Don't assume your client makes the connection by simply stating the benefits. For example, you can explain the cost-savings of an AFA and why it is an appropriate pricing solution. Discuss efficiencies that will result in adopting a particular process, the amount of time saved by following a new procedure, or how jointly identifying Key Performance Indicators will result in better service delivery. These outcomes are all measurable and thereby quantifiable, thus more believable. Focus on what they will gain in order to get their buy-in. Win themes are frequently articulated as benefits that the client will receive by hiring the law firm.

The solutions you have proposed must be backed up by tangible benefits that show you are the best firm for the project. You can be

Customer need/issue	Solution	Outcome/benefit	Proof
The client expects the law firm to provide a consolidated detailed invoice on a monthly basis to include all charges for all offices.	The client relationship partner will provide centralized invoicing services and review invoices from all offices working on the engagement. A consolidated invoice will be submitted to the in-house contact. The system is accessible real time to client and law firm to track status of billings immediately, 24/7. An administrator will be appointed as the "go-to" person on all invoices and be available to communicate day-to-day with your billing personnel. Software system ensures real-time access to invoices and expenses for review.	This system typically saves on average 20 percent of your accounting staff's time due to the ability to track invoices in real time. Thus, this process will save time and expense for your accounting department. The software system catalogs all expenses and information is available to client for instantaneous review and verification of individual invoices.	References from other law firm clients who use the system. Testimonials from satisfied clients. Accolades from the software system providers from third party users in the client's industry.

Figure 8.4: Overview of service to demonstrate understanding.

sure they will be asking themselves what the impact of your solutions will have on the company and what the risk is for following your solutions. Risk is always on the minds of buyers, no matter what the product or service. Purchasers of legal services are no exception and given the circumstance may be very high. A class action lawsuit can ruin a company's reputation and the company can suffer severe financial losses. While you cannot promise the outcome, you can explain the benefits your expertise and experience will bring and once again the proof that you have handled similar cases successfully before. Ask yourself the question "Why hire us?" The message being – for positive outcomes – hire us.

The role of legal procurement professionals was discussed in Chapter 1. Legal procurement views proposals as an opportunity to shed light on new client services. In addition to being objective when they recommend law firms, they are looking for added value services and appropriate AFAs, innovation, improved efficiency, and better processes.

"So what?"

Have you ever had anyone ask you, "So what?" a number of times while you are trying to explain something to them? It can be frustrating, right? Well, that is what I'm asking you to do when you brainstorm your benefit statements.

I find that the "So what?" test is a great way to verify whether the benefits proposed are actual benefits from the client's point of view. Ask "So what?" after every benefit. For example, often we state that a partner has 20 years of experience in a particular practice or industry. That is better than saying "extensive experience" (whatever that means). You need to ask what the significance of all those years of experience is and how it translates to your client at this particular time. Do the qualifications differentiate your team from the competition? You have assembled a great team and resources. So what? What does that mean to the client in the context of the RFP? Another reason why the "So what?" test is so effective is that you have to answer the question "Why?" "Why" validates your understanding of their needs/issues.

Asking "So what?" and "Why" will help you avoid boilerplate "So what?" So that you center your bid on strategies that matter to the client. Why? Because that is *all* that matters to the client.

As I said earlier, it is difficult to write about the client when you are asked to write about yourself. Use the "So what?" test to get yourself into the client's mindset. Ask this question after each benefit to see if you nailed it. This process will also help evaluators score you on what value you will bring to the organization.

The "So what?" test ties the proposal together. Make sure that you delve deeply into the "So what" test because you may need to ask "Why?" more than once to get to the core of the benefit. It can be frustrating, but at the end of the process you will have meaningful benefit statements that show you understand the important issues and that the benefits for hiring you are obvious.

Let's test it out:

- The client needs a global firm.
- We are a global firm. So what?
- We have offices in all the countries where you have offices. So what?
- Your client relationship partner – your central point of contact for this engagement – will be happy to introduce your legal team to a lawyer in one of our local offices. So what?
- You will have legal counsel with feet on the ground who possess valuable knowledge about the local legal system and business climate, as well as speak the local language to help you navigate in the legal environment. Can you think of any more "So what?" questions?

An example of asking "Why?" would be the following example:

Your local contact will coordinate with the client relationship partner. Why?

Answer: We have found that centralized communication is essential to a smooth running global engagement. Your client relations partner will coordinate with our global project management team to ensure that communications with your in-house team and our global lawyers are tracked to see that nothing falls through the cracks. Regular meetings with your point of contact and our team will make sure everyone is informed about key issues on a timely basis to keep the project on track.

Proof/evidence

Providing proof/evidence is the final step in this process. However, it is not the least important. This is where you prove that you can deliver the service you have promised. This is the confirmation that you have the right credentials and experience.

Proof encompasses:

1. Things you say about your firm;
2. Things your clients and vendors say about you; and
3. Third party comments.

They all play a role in proving you can make good on your promises. Proof needs to be dispersed throughout the proposal, but is often left out of the main body of the proposal, only put into bios, and left for the client to figure out if you really have the right credentials to address their needs/issues.

Things you say about your firm

Naturally, the first kind of proof – things you say about yourself – is not the most powerful body of proof. However, they are nevertheless important. Some examples would include:

- Setting precedents;
- Winning matters;
- Experience in the particular type of transaction;
- Relevant client lists (if the client name is not permitted you can mention the industry or relative size of the client, e.g. Fortune 500 company);
- Industry expertise;
- Lawyer rankings from credible sources;
- League tables;
- Project management methodology;
- Proprietary software;
- Diversity and inclusion policies;
- Pro bono work;
- Webinars;
- Podcasts;
- White papers on trending issues;
- Awards, including awards given by recognized industry associations and businesses;

- Speeches;
- Firm profile/ranking;
- Trade journal articles;
- Press releases; and
- Website.

Some law firms have articles about their alternative fee arrangement policies on their website. They describe AFAs that are about the sharing of risk and reward, their lawyers have "skin in the game" by offering an agreement that provides for the payment of fees, in part or in whole, depending on the outcome of a dispute. This information publicly demonstrates that the law firm means what it says and is confident that it can perform by upping the ante for a win and lessening the client's risk for a less desired outcome.

Things your clients and vendors say about your firm

The second kind of proof – the things your clients and vendors say about you – is strong evidence that you can really do what you claim. References from satisfied clients are a great way to back up your claims. Conversation with your clients are a great opportunity for prospective clients to ask questions about your service and confirm your credibility. Testimonials and quotes from clients in reputable legal directories such as *Chambers* can be put in text boxes at strategic points throughout the proposal. Case studies are a great way to promote your client and yourself. One firm put a case study on their website about outsourcing contracts, along with a quote from a client from *Chambers* about how happy the client was and an award they won from an external global sourcing organization. The firm flipped a summary of a matter into a case study. Brilliant!

Third party comments

The third kind of proof includes third party comments from reputable sources. For example, successful matters written about in newspapers or legal publications can be good publicity. Interviews with recognized legal publishers are also a good way of getting your message across. Awards, rankings, and analysts' reports from reliable sources are also a good testimony as to your capabilities.

After presenting all these kinds of proof, ask yourself if you would be convinced that you have the right credentials for the work product. If not, go back to the drawing board.

Summary

Figure 8.5 shows how needs, solutions, outcomes, and proof interconnect with each other in a different way to Figure 8.3. The left side focuses on what the client needs and the benefits the company will receive, and the right side focuses on your understanding of the needs and provides solutions that will successfully respond to the client needs and the proof that your firm is the right choice.

Client	Your firm
Needs/issues You are concerned with legal issues concerning diversity and inclusion (D&I) and want to broaden the skills of your in-house legal team regarding your policies. You also want to ensure that you are compliant.	**Solutions** We offer courses on the social and legal implications of diversity and inclusion (D&I) in the workplace at no cost to our clients. We also offer seminars to support human resources managers at no cost. We can also assist your in-house legal department and human resources department with up-to-date newsletters on D&I employment issues. Our website has regular blogs, webinars, and brochures featuring current legal issues on D&I.
Outcome/benefits Our clients have expressed that they have more confidence in handling D&I issues.	**Proof/evidence** Recently, we won a major D&I case for our client involving wrongful dismissal (describe relevant matter). We would be happy to refer you to our clients who have taken advantage of our courses on D&I issues. Recent topics that may interest you are: • Recent changes to legislation regarding D&I for in-house counsel; and • Human resources hiring issues that include D&I.

Figure 8.5: How needs, solutions, outcomes, and proof interconnect

Needs/issues, solutions, outcomes, and proof are the backbone of your strategy. It may take time to write good content for each step but in the end you will have a compelling proposal that will stand out from the competition.

Strategies to remember

1. Take into consideration legal procurement's goals for issuing the RFP;
2. Create win themes that will establish the strategic outline for your proposal;
3. Analyze needs, solutions, outcomes, and proof – apply strategy to each element; and
4. Verify the impact of your offer by asking if you would hire your firm if you were the client.

Chapter 9: Differentiation – the key to your strategy

I debated whether to include differentiation in the preceding chapter as differentiation is clearly a strategy and links back to needs, solutions, outcomes, and proof. However, I decided to make it a separate chapter so as to have it stand on its own merits.

A key differentiator can be defined as business attribute(s) and/or value that clearly separates it from the competition in a particular marketplace. Differentiators should be unique, measurable, and defendable. They can be made different by altering or moderating something. Differentiation must link to your value propositions. To be a true differentiator, competitors cannot say they have the same distinction.

Five to ten years ago I would have said that it would be difficult to differentiate law firms. That is not true today. The growth in technology is creating the need for legal services for rapidly growing areas such as artificial intelligence, blockchain, cybersecurity, cloud technology, and social media. Technology is also playing a fundamental role in law firms as they endeavor to create better efficiencies, processes, and pricing for their clients. Legal Project Management (LPM) is a growing specialty in law firms, as are pricing professionals. Corporate legal operations departments are becoming more sophisticated and developing technology to measure law firm performance, and law firms are creating technology to track data to match those needs. This leads to areas where law firms can differentiate themselves.

Many services that law firms tout as being differentiators are not in fact differentiators. Sometimes your offer is truly unique and sometimes it is how you implement the differentiator that makes it unique. When you are bidding for work, use differentials that will be meaningful to your client. Your service may in fact be unique amongst the firms proposing or in a certain geographical location so I wouldn't get hung up worrying about being the only law firm in the world to present services that you believe are a differentiator in the context of a particular RFP.

Differentiation strategy: questions to consider

- Is your service claim unique? Has a competitor beat you to the punch?
- Can you sustain your claim?
- Does your differentiation link back to needs/issues?
- Does your differentiation translate into meaningful benefits?
- Can you prove it is unique or has unique aspects that provide an added value to your client?

Services-based differentiation

Service-based differentiation involves stressing aspects of your service that differentiate your service deliverables. How innovative is your service offering? For example, one law firm released a mobile app that provides easy, consistent access to data breach statutes across the United States and jurisdictions, including Europe and Asia. Rather than sending out newsletters or email alerts they took it a step further, making their service offering unique.

Service that solves problems faster, or solves the same problem cheaper, is another differentiator. Outsourcing is becoming more common for law firms – either outsourcing services to a third party or providing services from a more economical internal service hub. For example, some firms have established a service center to support lawyers across their offices by providing services at a reduced cost with specialized expertise in corporate services, such as drafting and reviewing frequently recurring commercial documents; due diligence; and customary banking and security documentation. Once again, it is how the outsourcing is handled that can make it a differentiator.

How the technology was created can be a great way to separate your service offering from the competition. Ask your clients first if they'd use it. Apps are becoming a way to differentiate law firms, such as a Brexit app which provides updates on Brexit, an IP Health Check app which provides guidance on how companies can protect their intellectual property and related rights, and an app for news and information related to shale gas and hydraulic fracturing, including the latest industry trends and updates. A law firm with offices in Canada launched a chatbot powered by artificial intelligence that responds to questions about the mandatory Canadian data breach laws and new regulations that come into effect under the Personal Information Protection and Electronic Documents Act (PIPEDA). It will interactively guide clients through a conversation to determine if they need to consider reporting a data breach under Canadian privacy laws.

Many law firms have worked with their clients to create apps. Some law firms have partnered with industry experts to add credibility to their software systems; for example, Norton Rose Fulbright has gone live on SAP HANA with Fulcrum Global Technologies, and will consolidate five profit centers across the United Kingdom, United States, Canada, Australia, and South Africa. Will all of this technology bring in new clients? No, not necessarily, but it demonstrates that the firm understands the client's business needs and is creating services, many of them unique, to respond to them.

Needs/issues

Typical needs may include such issues as needing to improve business processes to improve efficiencies, save money, minimize risk, and improve operations. The Corporate Legal Operations Consortium (CLOC) 2018 conference identified several client needs.

An article by David Alkins, director of matter planning at Nixon Peabody LLP, and Lori Farrelly, director of management at Crowell & Moring LLP, was posted on the Legal Marketing Association Strategies blog posts, entitled *CLOC's Third Annual Corporate Legal Operations Institute: What Are Our Clients Thinking and Saying?*[1] The following information is taken from the article and edited by me as it relates to client needs and opportunities for differentiation:

What clients want

Compliance

Clients want increased compliance with their Outside Counsel Guidelines (OCGs), the documented specifications clients expect law firms to follow in providing legal services. Some corporations are now calling OCGs, Outside Counsel *Requirements*. The clients who are driving the evolution of the delivery of legal services are demanding consistency and adherence to their specifications. *Differentiate your firm by elaborating on a process you have developed to comply with your client's Outside Counsel Guidelines/Requirements.*

Communication and collaboration

Corporations want deeper, more dedicated and strategic relationships with fewer law firms. Fostering these relationships develops institutional knowledge about the corporation's business and allows for increased quality, predictability, efficiency, and value. In developing these relationships, law firms should focus on discussing, understanding and responding to the clients' pain points, priorities and aligning incentives. Legal Project Management/Planning (LPM) is becoming an important differentiator as it often addresses pain points, and sets priorities for matters by scoping and scheduling projects. You need to communicate with your client to learn what they consider to be a differentiator in their situation. LPM provides benefits and there is proof that it works for the client and law firm. It creates a win/win scenario. When law firms employ LPM there are fewer write-offs and proper management of matters avoids difficult conversations with procurement when things go off the rails because the project was not scoped correctly.

It is also a great conversation tool that truly solves your clients' issues. It makes sure matters are "right staffed" by first completing a project plan. *Planning the engagement is really a gold mine for law firms because it allows you to get valuable information from your client that you may not ordinarily have access to.*

Diversity

Clients want to hire diverse teams as part of the core values of their organization, but also because those teams are proven to be more innovative, efficient, and likely to achieve desired results. There is opportunity for outside counsel to achieve a competitive edge by focusing on diversity and inclusion programs.

Data

Many in-house legal operations teams are developing dashboards and reporting tools (at varying degrees of sophistication), in part to evaluate the law firms they are working with, by rating them by a variety of metrics. Differentiate your firm by sharing your data with your clients and use it to start those important conversations.

Once you have decided on differentiators specific to your client you can concentrate on how you can differentiate your firm around the solutions you propose.

Solutions

Solutions are what the client is looking for by hiring an expert. I know we can't call lawyers "experts," but in this case I will. Your solution may not always be able to be defined in the true sense as unique, but coupled with the impacts or benefits your solution will have on your client's business, it could be. Your solutions relate back to the needs or the specific situation your client faces.

A solution that involves technology can be a differentiator within itself. A great way to show that your technology solution has credibility is to partner with a recognized technology company. One law firm announced plans to collaborate on the development of a new software platform to deliver improved cost-effectiveness, promote pricing certainty, and optimize workflows and staffing by standardizing metrics for legal services. The system is powered by IBM's comprehensive predictive analytics system, SPSS, and running on IBM Cloud. Not only did the firm create a software solution to respond to a common need of clients, they partnered with a credible company to create the solution. This is a good example of where needs, solutions, outcomes/benefits, and proof interconnect.

Outcomes/benefits

Outcomes/benefits are only meaningful if you know which benefits mean the most to your client, such as performance standards that can be measured, operational efficiency, and value for money. This may not be possible if you are responding to an RFP for a company that you are unfamiliar with but you can predict the value by analyzing what your existing clients consider as providing true value. For example, some firms have created an automatic feedback system for all matters. My guess is that many clients would like access to this kind of feedback mechanism. Remember that by asking "So what?" you can turn your lawyers into legal advisors with insight.

The reasons *why* and *how* you do something can be a bigger differentiator than *what* you do.

Proof

Proof that you can deliver is established by the team you proposed in the proposal. Lawyers and other professionals who work at your firm can be differentiators. This is when lawyers' credentials are important. They need to stand out as front-runners in a particular industry and leaders in their practice area. Customized bios are an important part of your proof that you have selected the right person to respond to the criteria of the RFP.

Let's take legal project management as an example. A global firm has a director of project management and legal innovation who also teaches a class on "Legal Project/Practice Management" at the University of

Calgary's Law School. While LPM is not necessarily a differentiator in itself, the fact that the director teaches a university course on the subject certainly is.

I have mentioned the benefits of competitor research and proposal debriefs throughout this book. Here is another example of where they pay off. Ask your clients where you rank vis-à-vis your competitors in, for example, innovation, service delivery, technology, processes, efficiencies, and cost savings. Where you rank high, use this information as proof that you can deliver on your promises.

Added value

I recently moderated a Thomson Reuters panel discussion, "The Price is Right: Mastering Client Value Propositions in Legal Practice", with corporate purchasers of legal services and knowledgeable pricing professionals from law firms. One fact was emphasized throughout the conference: one size does not fit all. If your client does not see your offering as adding value to their company, they will not accept it. This goes for technology solutions too. The shiny object you created may not mean anything to all clients. Once again, you need to carefully verify the needs and benefits with your client. You may need the system to be flexible enough to be customized. Before your firm spends a lot of time and money creating software solutions you need to find out if they want them. A pilot project is preferable to a big launch, then failing and losing credibility with your clients and the marketplace.

Particularly if your clients are high technology companies you need to keep up with the latest trends and technologies, or your clients may shift to other law firms for their competitive technology. A lawyer at Microsoft mentioned that as they are a technology company, they expect their law firms to be tech savvy and creative when it comes to creating technology services. Other companies mentioned that lawyers need to be tech savvy by learning the company's technology such as their e-billing system.

Corporations represented at the conference said that clients are often driving change because law firms fail to do so and more companies are bringing more work in-house and setting up a legal operations department.

I met Lucy Endel Bassli when she was a panelist at the session I moderated, "High Noon: A Pricing Negotiation Master Class", at the 24th Annual Marketing Partner Forum. Lucy voiced many opinions on how law firms could provide better pricing alternatives to their clients.

Until recently, she was assistant general counsel at Microsoft. In 2018, she founded InnoLegal Services and serves as chief legal strategist for LawGeex.

Bassli posted the article, *The Legal Ecosystem: The Regulators and the Do'ers Part 2*, on Thomson Reuters, Legal Executive Institute,[2] where she wrote:

> *"The sheer number of people identified as legal innovators, disruptors and futurists, coupled with the growing number of legal roles with the word innovation in the title, demonstrates that these changes are a natural outgrowth of legal professionals seeking creative new solutions to age-old problems.*
>
> *"Without getting too philosophical, let's look at how these industry groups are influencing the legal industry today. No other player in the ecosystem has had a more vocal impact recently than groups like CLOC and ACC Legal Ops. No doubt, if you are reading this article, you have heard of CLOC. That is due to the fast-paced rise of legal operations professionals across the industry. In firms or corporations, the role of legal ops professionals has evolved and transformed the definition of legal services in recent years.*
>
> *"These industry groups are bringing together operationally-minded lawyers with business and operations experts to gather, share ideas, and demand change in the industry. As corporate legal operations specialists have shared and adopted successful tactics and processes, there has been a seismic shift across the ecosystem. Law firms are hearing requests for similar approaches and increased efficiencies from different corporate clients; while legal tech successes and failures are being openly discussed, and references from trusted colleagues remain critical for successful implementations."*

As I mentioned in Chapter 1, many in-house legal operations teams are developing software to track law firms and individual lawyer's performance, and pricing promises, and using reporting tools to rate their legal service providers on a variety of metrics.

Image differentiation – branding

One more kind of differentiation that bears mentioning is image differentiation or branding. Acritas publishes an annual Law Firm Brand Index that rates various attributes of law firm branding. Your image or reputation is one way your client and the marketplace perceive your firm and its services. Your brand positions your firm; for example, some firms are identified by being a member of the magic circle, AM Law 100, or seven sisters (Canada).

Negative strategies and positive strategies

There are two other strategies that can be used to differentiate your law firm: negative strategies and positive strategies. Negative strategies can be used to show that you understand your client's pain, and positive strategies show the benefits of working with you.

Negative strategies = fear

Negative strategies demonstrate a fear, or something the client wants to avoid. This relates to client needs/issues and solutions.

Remember the American Express ads, "Don't leave home without it"? This is an excellent example of a fear campaign. This series of ads showed what could happen if your credit card was lost or stolen, particularly while on vacation. Celebrities entertained audiences by acting out fear-provoking experiences and how American Express saved them. Can you build some legitimate fear tactics into your proposal? For example, can you discuss risk that is embedded in new legislation and provide risk mitigation tactics? Let your client see that you understand their pain and provide viable solutions.

Positive strategies = gain

Positive strategies demonstrate what is to be gained by following your advice. This relates to solutions and benefits. This approach seeks ways to create win/win strategies by aligning strategies with the needs/issues and providing feasible solutions and benefits.

L'Oreal's slogan, "Because I'm worth it" makes it about the person. Bids that make it about the client and deliver benefits get the client's buy-in.

In summary, I would like to draw your attention to an article that validates all the points I have emphasized about how needs, solutions, outcomes, proof, and differentiators are intertwined. In the May 2018 issue of *Forum*, Thomson Reuters, Susan Raridon Lambreth, a founding principal at LawVision Group interviewed Stéphanie Hamon, managing director, head of external engagement, legal at Barclays, about creating successful panel relationships.[3] Lambreth asked, "How do you evaluate your outside counsel?" Here is Hamon's response:

"Barclays created a capability framework we call 'Expectations of Law Firms' with objectives under each capability. These are included in a scorecard that is used in ongoing assessments of panel firms with evaluations at the end of each matter and each quarter. The four categories are as follows:

1. *Legal advice – offer excellent technical legal advice, quality control, incorporating collective experience across the firm (not just individuals servicing the matter), and bring a strategic approach to legal matters;*
2. *Collaboration – operate as an extension of the in-house team, working collaboratively with other Barclays outside firms, capturing knowledge across the firm to provide value to Barclays;*
3. *Value for money – provide accurate cost estimates and understand the cost drivers and most efficient approaches for matters; offer alternative fee arrangements (AFAs); and*
4. *Thought leadership – provide advice based on innovation and changes in the industry to enhance quality of work and service to Barclays and help us deliver to our strategy.*

"This year, two new categories of Innovation and Technology will be added.

"In addition, a new part of the Value for Money category will be Effective Fee Arrangements (EFAs) because not every AFA is a good solution for Barclays. We have lots of data about the cost of services so we usually have a ballpark number for each legal area. We are developing a "cost catalog" for common areas like a witness interview in an investigation or due diligence for a simple M&A transaction.

"Barclays shares a lot of financial data and other metrics, and we also provide a lot of qualitative feedback in a bid to encourage transparency. We want the firms to know where they stand in rankings and ratings. We share a scattergram with each firm that shows their position relative to the other panel firms (though not identifying the other firms).

"We see legal project management (LPM) at the core of all service delivery. It means clear understanding of the matter at the outset, clear scoping of the work ... it is the foundation of everything. It means having the right stakeholders involved, ensuring the right deliverables and the right fees for the value of the matter. Right now, LPM is very much a differentiating factor where proactive firms have an advantage

with it … and probably will be for the next two years. Then, I expect others will catch up."

Needs/issues, solutions, outcomes/benefits, and proof are important differentiators that can add value to your clients and help you win bids if you can articulate them using this formula.

Strategies to remember

1. Differentiation is key to your strategy;
2. Competitive analysis is key to identifying differentiators;
3. Why and how you provide your services can be a differentiator; and
4. Needs/issues, solutions, outcomes, and proof are linked together to demonstrate differentiation.

Reference

1. http://blog.legalmarketing.org/clocs-third-annual-corporate-legal-operations-institute-what-are-our-clients-thinking-and-saying
2. http://www.legalexecutiveinstitute.com/legal-ecosystem-regulators-doers-part-2/
3. https://blogs.thomsonreuters.com/answerson/an-interview-with-barclays-stephanie-hamon/

Chapter 10: Writing a strategic executive summary

The executive summary is indisputably one of the most important components of your proposal. The summary is the first thing that is read – by everyone including the c-suite. Quickly followed by the fee section. If your summary does not say what matters to the client then your proposal will be perceived as generic and meaningless to the decision-makers.

The purpose of the summary is to show why your firm is the best choice – not repeating everything in the proposal. When it comes right down to it, it's not really about summarizing the proposal at all, it is about convincing management that you are the right choice. Follow the selection criteria and the formula for the needs, solutions, benefits, proof, and differentiation.

The highest score wins

Before you start writing, check the evaluation criteria to make sure your strategies are aligned with the criteria. As with everything in responding to a formal RFP, you need to follow the instructions. To fail to do so could make your proposal non-compliant. If the RFP says the executive summary should provide certain information, provide it.

When clients give you the evaluation criteria, particularly if it is weighted, it is a gift. Don't look this gift horse in the mouth. Use it to decide where to put the emphasis. As I said before, I look at proposals as a process of elimination. The highest score wins. So, pay close attention to the evaluation criteria and weightings and use it as a guide. Repeat the vocabulary of the RFP and selection criteria to help evaluators zero in on your key points. Everything you write must be considered in the context of the evaluation criteria in order to maximize your score.

The opening paragraph needs to grab their attention. It should not be a list of superlatives that have no real value to the client. Your summary should explain what your recommendations and qualifications add up to for them. The details are in the proposal. If you are the incumbent you can customize your summary with your top achievements and use your inside knowledge to nail the issues and how you can help.

Some proposal specialists recommend that the executive summary be written first. In a perfect world, the executive summary sets up the strategy for the proposal. Others recommend that it be written last, hitting the main points of the proposal. I am going to say at this point that both are right. Time permitting, I like to write an outline of the executive summary with the win themes and other strategies to map out the selling points before the proposal is set in stone. Then go back and flesh out the content that is developed around needs, solutions, benefits, proof, and differentiators.

I find that by leaving the executive summary to the end you risk running out of time and can end up with an overblown cover letter that misses the substantive reasons as to why they should hire you.

Recently, I wrote an executive summary for a P3 proposal that was going to state legislature, so it had to be perfect. Because of the tight deadline, I ended up writing it in the middle of the proposal process and adding differentiators at the end. So, I guess what I am saying is there are "best practices" and then there is doing what you can to hit your deadlines. Don't get fixated on when to write the summary, just make sure it contains the right elements.

I put the chapter on executive summaries near the end of my book because I wanted to cover strategies for needs, solutions, benefits, proof, and differentiators before tackling executive summaries, because this is central to winning.

Some RFPs do not call for an executive summary; however, unless they prohibit a summary, I recommend that you include one, even if it is not scored. If you are only allowed a cover letter, then write it like a mini summary.

Needs/issues – you get it

Start your executive summary from the client's perspective, accentuating the benefits they will get by buying your services. That means addressing their needs/issues in such a way as to show that you understand their situation and concerns and, if relevant, their pain points. The summary needs to be convincing and highlight the benefits of hiring your firm.

You can't solve a problem that you don't understand. Before a client appoints you, they need to know that you understand their needs/issues. Point out important considerations, including things that are not addressed in the RFP, that demonstrate your grasp of the situation.

To demonstrate your understanding, show insight about the issue or problem that the client may not have considered or be aware of.

The solution – you've got it

Decision-makers need to understand your solution to their needs and how it will benefit their business. Even though your information is presented at a high level, you need to convince the client that you have come up with the best advice. The specifics come later in the proposal.

If appropriate, talk about your approach to fees and AFAs. Many firms prefer not to discuss fees in the summary and if the proposal is split between technical and financial submissions, you won't be able to. However, if you can, refer to some of your approaches to AFAs as benefits or differentiators. You know it is important, so present them in a positive light. Leave the details for the proposal.

The outcome/benefit – you define it

I work with many law firms and can assure you that the proposing law firms will offer the same basic services. Consider the positive outcomes your solution will provide. If the proposal is for a typical legal service, then perhaps how you deliver it will be important to the client, or maybe your AFAs are superior or managed better. Show how the client will benefit by hiring your firm.

I see the statement "we will be your trusted advisor" in many proposals. What does it mean to be a trusted advisor when you are unknown to the company? Trust and credibility are sometimes listed as synonyms. However, literature shows that trust must be earned. Credibility results from proving your claims. You need to show benefits for what you have proposed to become a trusted advisor. If your firm is the incumbent, you may be able to say that you have been a trusted advisor and give examples.

The proof/evidence – you can do it

Unsubstantiated claims can backfire if you can't back them up. Here is your opportunity to prove you can deliver what you have promised. This establishes your credibility.

The credentials of your client services team are one way you can prove what you say is true. Explain why your qualifications matter and what the client will get as a result. Credentials for each team member should speak for themselves as a standalone piece. Provide relevant experience, emphasizing client engagements and matters, expertise in the industry and practice area for all on the team, including associates. If your team members' bios do not show relevance to the needs, solutions, and benefits, revise them. They need to be customized to match the RFP requirements. *Relevant* being the operative word.

By explaining the role each team member will play and their experience in carrying out similar roles for other corporations, you build credibility and confidence that you can do what you promise; for example, if it is a global bid, your point-of-contact partner's experience managing large, complex global engagements that are similar to the one you are bidding on will be vital. How the client relationship partner will manage the team, the benefit of your process, bringing the team up to speed at no cost to the client, client meetings, performance reviews, and KPIs can all be recapped in this section.

Describing the role of each team member will define how your service will be delivered. If LPM professionals are on staff, the benefits of their role can be used to explain how the matter will be scoped, managed, and reported on. A simple graphic would be good to show how your team and the corporation's team will work together, and how the function of LPM will be coordinated, particularly if the corporation has a legal operations department. Detailed organization charts and graphics will be in the body of the proposal.

RFPs typically ask for a description of your firm. They don't want a regurgitation of your website, they want what's relevant to them. If the client is a global corporation but is only asking for services in a specific geographical location, focus on your strengths in that location, your local team, knowledge of the local laws and business environment. Skip the verbiage about all your global qualifications that do not provide value within the confines of the RFP. Of course, if you have a process to manage global companies, you should mention the benefits to the client, but only within the scope of what you've been asked.

Use evidence to back up why your firm is the best choice by providing references, testimonials, awards, books, and industry speaking engagements. Only relevant information should be included, not a laundry list of accolades.

Differentiators – you can always differentiate

You can't be "unique" if you are not different. A summary that sounds like all the others will not draw the attention of decision-makers. If you can explain why and how your differentiators set a new standard in client service and pricing, then why wouldn't they choose your firm?

Strategies to remember

1. Use the evaluation criteria as your guide to strategy;
2. Follow the formula: needs, solutions, benefits, proof;
3. Explain what differentiates your firm from the competition; and
4. Include only relevant information.

Chapter 11:
Effectively using red teams to verify strategies

I am a firm believer in using red teams to increase the chances of winning. They are often difficult to arrange at law firms, but are definitely worth the effort. I have never had a red team review where the team did not contribute insightful comments for improving the proposal. It is difficult to see the forest for the trees when the proposal team is in the thick of a bid. An objective review of the proposal by knowledgeable partners is worth its weight in gold.

I think the colored teaming method can get a bit out of hand. For example, there is the pink team, red team, green team, gold team, and some companies have added a blue and a purple team. I am not saying that the processes behind the teams are not important. However, trying to cram in all these teams into a short turnaround bid is not possible and can be counterproductive. In my experience, a red team is sufficient if it is done well.

I have suggested some alternatives to a formal red team review in this chapter, should a full-blown red team not be possible or practical. I do, however, recommend that some form of assessment take place to cement your strategies and increase your win rate.

Right people – right thing – right time

As with so any things in life, having the right people doing the right thing at the right time is the key to success. Proposals are no exception. As this book is centered on strategy, this principle applies to red teams if you want to get the full benefit of their advice.

Role of the red team

Essentially, the red team assumes the role of the corporate selection committee. The team evaluates the proposal, scores the content using evaluation criteria, recommends improvements, and most importantly provides input on how to resolve any issues. The team provides an objective view of the proposal to make sure it meets the client's criteria.

If the RFP does not contain formal evaluation criteria you can make up your own evaluation criteria by having the reviewers score each section on a scale of one to five, whereby one = needs improvement, and five = very good.

Trying to score a proposal without reading the RFP is like trying to mark an examination paper without the exam questions. It is important that the red team read the RFP prior to evaluating the proposal to make sure the answers contain the best content.

The proposal needs to demonstrate the magic formula, and based on these criteria the red team needs to determine if you have proven that your firm is the right choice:

1. Needs/issues;
2. Solution;
3. Outcomes/benefits;
4. Proof/evidence; and
5. Differentiators.

In order to score a proposal properly, the team must have a good understanding of the client's requirements. They will use the selection evaluation criteria provided by the client or the criteria supplied by the proposal manager to score the proposal.

The team will run through the "So what?" test to identify any weaknesses, document content requiring clarification, identify any gaps, and evaluate win themes/strategies. They will also note whether the proposal projects excitement/interest in the engagement.

Right people

The red team needs to be selected early in the process and the meetings should be listed on the timeline schedule that is distributed following the kick-off meeting. This also serves to let the proposal team know that senior management will be reviewing the proposal so that deadlines are adhered to.

It is essential to select the right team members. The lead partner and proposal manager are often the best to recommend the members of the red team. The lead partner knows who has the specific expertise that would make a good reviewer, and the proposal manager knows who has performed well on previous red teams and provided good input. Personal biases and personalities also need to be considered.

I have found that the managing partner or CEO are often a good choice for significant bids as they have access to additional information, know the big picture of the firm, and can offer an objective opinion. CEOs and managing partners will not likely be available, nor should they be, on all bids that require a red team, but it is still important to choose a senior, knowledgeable team for the review.

The red team should not include members who are on the proposal team as you want to get an objective viewpoint – a "fresh perspective". The most important participant of a red team is the team manager. The red team needs a leader to drive the process. The red team should not be too big so as to make it unwieldly. The team should include:

- CEO/managing partner (if appropriate);
- Partner with industry expertise;
- Senior practice area partner; and
- Lawyer who knows the client (if possible).

I recommend that the pricing decision-makers and pricing team arrange a separate approval meeting along with the lead partner. Pricing follows another process and often a different management committee. Once pricing comes up in the conversation, everything goes off the rails and it is hard to get the proposal assessment team back on track.

When the entire team follows the same process, their contribution will be easy to implement. Using the same process will make the input consistent, making it easier for the proposal team to identify where to make changes. It is best when the red team can meet together as ideas can be discussed and it will prevent conflicting points of view. If this is not possible, have the red team members send their comments and scoring to the lead partner and proposal manager.

Right thing

It is important to review the right thing. The checklist shown in Figure 11.1 is a guide that the red team can use to focus on the right kind of information to be reviewed. Many of the steps focus on important strategies to make certain that you get to the heart of the matter.

Role of the proposal manager

The proposal manager will send the following information to the red team to let them know what is expected of them:

- Instructions for the team:
- Role of team and section(s) to review.
- Briefing document:
- Company/name of person issuing RFP;
- Client objective(s);
- Reason for bidding;
- Background on company;
- Industry;
- Practice areas;
- Bid team;
- Red team;
- Proposal manager;
- Deadline for submission;
- RFP;
- Copy of the evaluation criteria, even if it is in the RFP;
- Win themes/strategies; and
- Deadline for comments.

Figure 11.1: Red team review checklist

Right time

When to review the proposal is a critical part of the process. It should be on the timeline schedule from the beginning. The proposal for the red team should be the "final" draft. However, given tight timeframes, the chances that the final version will be ready are rare to none.

If you wait for the "perfect" draft you may run out of time for the red team to review the bid, make recommendations, and fix the proposal.

Produce a close-to-final draft that is aesthetically pleasing and that has been proofread – or at least run through spell checker. As discussed earlier, if there are typos or grammatical errors in the draft, the lawyers will start editing the proposal (occupational hazard) and not focus on the big picture.

Alternatives to formal red team reviews

If you are under a tight schedule you may need to resort to some of the following people to get input into your proposal (with the lead partner's permission):

1. **Partners** – ask a senior partner in a particular practice area or an industry group to review relevant content;
2. **Associates** – ask them to review the proposal. They often know the company, industry, or matters so they can provide valuable input; don't discount them out of hand;
3. **Proposal team** – ask if anyone has written a proposal for the industry to review your proposal. They may have some relevant content that can be customized;
4. **Business development manager** – ask the manager to read the proposal to make sure you haven't missed anything; and
5. **Client services manager** – I am trusting that the client manager is already on the proposal team if the RFP is from an existing client. If the manager is not available, then you can ask for approval to speak with another member of the team to check the validity of your propositions.

Following the red team review

A copy of the proposal will be created with comments from the red team (likely in track changes).

Following the red team review, there are several ways that the team can share their comments and recommendations. I find meeting with the red team along with the lead partner to be a good process. The entire proposal team does not need to be in the meeting as it will become too cumbersome.

The proposal team should meet with the lead lawyer and the proposal manager to review the red team's input and follow-up on the actions to be taken. The red team should assist the proposal team in making recommended changes. In the end, it is usually the lead partner who makes the final decision as to the content to include in the proposal.

Red team review: general information

Process:

- Review RFP;
- Review briefing document;
- Review selection criteria;
- Review proposal section assigned;
- Write comments in the margins or at the end of sections; and
- Complete red team review checklist.

Role of red team:

- Assume the role of the selection committee, evaluate the proposal from the point of view of the client (use RFP evaluation criteria if available);
- Identify any problems, errors, gaps; and
- Make recommendation(s) on how to resolve the issues.

Red team review: checklist

Key: 1 – Rewrite; 2 – Needs improvement; 3 – Adequate; 4 – Good; 5 – Very good

Meets all requirements in the RFP	1	2	3	4	5
Suggestions for improvement:					
Is it convincing?	1	2	3	4	5
Suggestions for improvement:					
Demonstrates a clear understanding of the client's problems/issues	1	2	3	4	5
Suggestions for improvement:					
Demonstrates understanding of the client's business	1	2	3	4	5
Suggestions for improvement:					
Demonstrates understanding of the client's industry	1	2	3	4	5
Suggestions for improvement:					

Figure 11.2: Red team review

Demonstrates understanding of the client's industry	1	2	3	4	5
Suggestions for improvement:					
Identifies solutions and how they benefit the client	1	2	3	4	5
Suggestions for improvement:					
Identifies firm's strengths and how they benefit the client	1	2	3	4	5
Suggestions for improvement:					
Discusses specific outcomes/benefits and how they benefit the client	1	2	3	4	5
Suggestions for improvement:					
Win theme(s) is/are clear and valued by the client	1	2	3	4	5
Suggestions for improvement:					
Writing is clear and easy to follow	1	2	3	4	5
Suggestions for improvement:					
Substantiates claims with proof/ evidence (past experience, etc.)	1	2	3	4	5
Suggestions for improvement:					
Describes differentiators that matter to the client	1	2	3	4	5
Suggestions for improvement:					
Clearly demonstrates why the client should choose your firm?	1	2	3	4	5
Suggestions for improvement:					

Sign-off

Signature: Print name:

Date:

Strategies to remember

1. Choose the right people – who will add strategic insight;
2. Do the right thing – review the proposal to verify/improve winning strategies;
3. Pick the right time – review as close to the final draft as possible to get the best input;
4. Ensure you follow the formula: needs, solutions, benefits, proof; and
5. Include your differentiators.

Chapter 12:
Strategic proposal tracking

The number and complexity of RFPs is growing. I have noticed that even smaller firms are now being asked to respond to RFPs to keep their business with long-standing clients. Law firms invest more and more lawyer time – including senior lawyer time – on bids and in our environment, time is literally money. Senior partners required for certain approvals also need to be added to the mix. Add to that the time and expense of the pricing team, LPM, proposal managers, and other SMEs. Responding to RFPs is expensive.

Most firms do some reporting on proposal wins and losses. However, few analyze the reasons for their wins and losses, so they keep repeating the same mistakes. Einstein is credited as saying "Insanity is doing the same thing over and over again and expecting different results". It is important to track your proposal results and analyze your wins/losses to identify your strengths and weaknesses to improve your win rate.

Of course, if you do not follow a strict go/no-go process (chapter 2) your results will be skewed because you will be including RFPs that you did not have a chance of winning along with real opportunities, making your performance look worse than it is.

Measuring win rates

There are two primary ways that win rates are measured:

1. Comparing the number of proposals submitted vs the number of wins and losses: win ratio; and
2. Adding the total revenue won with the total dollar amount bid on: ratio of revenue bid to revenue gained.

Having said that, the fee quoted in the proposal does not always reflect the revenue we end up with – sometimes it is more, sometimes less.

When producing win/loss reports you need to make sure that your figures reflect the whole story. The more variables for the reasons for the win/loss, the better your analysis will be and the more meaningful your won/lost report will be.

Statistics can be broken down by:

- Incumbent vs new client wins/losses;
- Total wins and total dollar value won per lead partner and proposal team;
- Win ratio by industry;
- Win ratio by service areas;
- Win ratio by office;
- Mandates/transaction RFPs compared with full blown RFPs;
- RFPs compared with the results from solicited and unsolicited pitches;
- Ratio of the cost to win (cost of non-billable lawyer time, proposal team, and SMEs salaries); and
- Win ratio by pricing and AFAs.

Proposals can also be measured by process improvements as they relate to time reduced to produce a proposal. This can be measured by dollars saved (salary and/or chargeable time). This might include a proposal software system.

Proposals are a moving target, so reports should be issued monthly, month-over-month, and year-over-year to catch any irregularities (such as a drop in the number of RFPs; if you are getting fewer you need to find out why).

If you collect the right metrics you will begin to see a pattern emerge that will help you understand when or why you win or lose. You need to look at your win/loss statistics holistically to see the relationship between your won/lost rate and the reasons why you won or lost. Once you have narrowed it down you will know how to leverage your strengths and diminish your weaknesses on competitive bids.

You need to drill down to the causes for your wins and losses. Some firms approach client debriefs as an ad hoc activity and do not conduct an in-depth analysis of the reasons for the win/loss, thus it is a wasted exercise. A detailed analysis can reveal strengths to be capitalized on and weaknesses that can be mitigated. This should not turn into a finger pointing exercise. The analysis can be used to develop strategies to improve your results.

Month over month

Date received	Due date	Type of document (RFP, RFI, RFQ)	Office	Company Client yes/no	Industry(s)	Practice area(s)	Opportunity

Lead partner	Proposal manager	SMEs	Kind of fee	Estimated fee	Win/loss	Who won	Debrief input

Lawyer team hours

Quarter over quarter

Date received	Due date	Type of document (RFP, RFI, RFQ)	Office	Company Client yes/no	Industry(s)	Practice area(s)	Opportunity

Lead partner	Proposal manager	SMEs	Kind of fee	Estimated fee	Win/loss	Who won	Debrief input

Lawyer team hours

Year over year

Date received	Due date	Type of document (RFP, RFI, RFQ)	Office	Company Client yes/no	Industry(s)	Practice area(s)	Opportunity

Lead partner	Proposal manager	SMEs	Kind of fee	Estimated fee	Win/loss	Who won	Debrief input

Lawyer team hours

Figure 12.1: Proposal tracker

The tracking information in Figure 12.1 can be put into an Excel document for analysis and producing won/lost reports. Reports can be produced by month, quarter, and year.

Analyzing your wins and losses is an important strategy. Delve deep into the data and comments from debriefs and use this information to strengthen your weaknesses and capitalize on your strengths.

Strategies to remember

1. Use the go/no-go process to respond to only RFPs you can win;
2. Track wins/losses to uncover strategies; and
3. Analyze won/lost debriefs to reveal strengths and weaknesses.

www.ingramcontent.com/pod-product-compliance
Ingram Content Group UK Ltd.
Pitfield, Milton Keynes, MK11 3LW, UK
UKHW021849150926
8657IPUK00005B/152

9 781783 583362